THE
FLIP
SIDE
of SOUL

THE
FLIP
SIDE
of SOUL

Letters to My Son

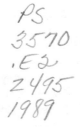

BOB
TEAGUE

William Morrow and Company, Inc.
New York

Library of Congress Cataloging-in-Publication Data

Teague, Bob.
   The flip side of soul.

   1. Teague, Bob—Correspondence. 2. Authors, American—20th century—Correspondence. 3. Journalists—United States—Correspondence. 4. Fathers and sons—United States. 5. United States—Race relations. 6. Afro-Americans. I. Title.
PS3570.E2Z495 1989   305.8'96073   88-31707
ISBN 0-688-08260-2

Printed in the United States of America

First Edition

1 2 3 4 5 6 7 8 9 10

BOOK DESIGN BY JAYE ZIMET

"If I were a black man, I'd be living in a state of constant fury."
—WESTBROOK PEGLER

"I'm trying to cut down on fury myself. Bad for digestion. Am thinking of switching to finesse."
—BOB TEAGUE

DEAR ADAM
MY SON:

As I write this letter, alone in my apartment, I scarcely can believe that this night in September '87 is the eve of your twenty-first birthday. A sobering side effect of my late fifties. Obviously, the world has flip-flopped a bunch of times since I wrote *Letters* in '68. Though addressed to you, the thoughts I wanted to convey were meant for all youngsters growing up black or white in our ineffably racist society. You were only twenty-two months old. I had no guarantee that I would survive the turbulent sixties. A perilous era. More than a few brave and angry blacks and whites were standing on their hind legs fighting for racial equality. Some were killed. Many others suffered crippling wounds to the body, permanent damage to the soul. As for me, I managed to succeed in my profession by really trying. I prospered. I also had a high old time which continues. Lucky me. During thirty-one years as a print, radio, and TV journalist in New York City, very few of the newsmakers I have covered struck me as being luckier or happier with their lots. How and why I have reached such an enviable plateau is terribly important, I believe, to explain for whom it may concern. Yes, I dare to boast: I have grown during these past two decades—far beyond the modest goals I had set for myself in a distant ghetto long ago. Not the least of my more recent accomplishments is an ability to think and feel beyond the imperatives that come with being black. What a relief. New reasons to rejoice, to hope and dare. All of which add up to a major compensation for growing older: Life is less of a hassle.

Hence, my initial decision in '68 to prepare a legacy of letters. My purpose then was the same as now in these 1987–88 additions, retractions, and trepidations: An urgent need to alert you. My theory is, if you can pick up some clues of what reality is like early on, before it crashes in unannounced, you may not be caught so totally off guard—unprepared and undone—as most men are.

Being the cool and independent spirit that you have lately proved to be, you may feel that you already know the score. Or certainly a helluva lot more than your old man gives you credit for, right? What you think in that respect, Adam, is somewhat true. Which does not, however, explode my belief that I have examined more pieces of the puzzle than almost anyone your age. You want proof? Okay. Right now, only a few steps from the threshold of senior citizenship, I am my own best friend. As a younger man, I had been my own worst enemy. I have finally kicked the habit of working against myself. Cold turkey. Sadly, though, I first suffered an embarrassing gamut of trial and error.

Let me back up for a moment. I should have said "myselves" a few sentences ago. It is at last apparent to me that there always have been at least seven conflicting egos inside the aging apparatus known to you as Dad. Virtually everything else I will tell you in the pages ahead relates in some way to what I say here: I have accepted my kaleidoscopic selves. Regularly, I make a conscious effort to give each one of my guys an hour or two in the spotlight.

A very special woman, Lady Jan, has graciously accompanied me on this odyssey into higher awareness. In fact, I doubt that I could have come so far without the lady who has replaced your mother in my heart. Ah, but that is another matter—relevant though peripheral here—which I shall address in due time. First, let me unload the heavy stuff . . .

TO MY SON ADAM, THE FORMER EIGHT-YEAR-OLD STAR QUARTERBACK IN THE KNUTE ROCKNE LEAGUE:

Watching a gridiron disaster on the tube yesterday—Wisconsin losing to Northwestern, ugh!—I happily reprised a personal epiphany: My very first perfect finesse. Which spawned side effects that gave your dad a big head start toward success after graduation.

It happened in a football triumph—Wisconsin over Northwestern in 1949, my senior year on the varsity. As our team was suiting up in the visitors' dressing room at Dyche Stadium, Evanston, Illinois, that crisp October Saturday, a black Northwestern senior sneaked in to warn me, "They know about your back injury. They're all going after it right off the bat. After what you did to Indiana last week, they figure the only way to beat the Badgers is to knock you out of the game." His motive was not to undermine the Wildcats' game plan; he simply wanted to protect a rare species of that era—a black running back in the Big Ten conference. "So watch your ass out there. Good luck."

He was gone before I could thank him. My heartbeat was faltering in overdrive. Despite a special spongy rubber pad our trainer had devised to cover the deep bruise in the lower left side of my back, I couldn't possibly stand up to the heavy-handed tricks those Neanderthal guards and tackles had in mind. How the hell had they discovered my painful secret? Not a word about it had appeared on any sports page during the week. In fact, our coach had barred the media from our practice sessions so that my cautious participation—no full-speed contact drills—would not be reported to the enemy. Nor had there been any published speculation about my limping exit, after scoring three touchdowns, late in the fourth quarter of the Indiana game. Nevertheless, some spy had given me away.

As I taped the special pad over my Achillean vulnerability, I felt depressed, picturing myself being carried off the field on a stretcher. No other scenario made sense; they would zero in on that telltale bulge under my jersey and— Hey, wait a minute. What if the telltale bulge was on the other side of my back?

On our first play from scrimmage, I took a hand-off from the quarterback and slammed into a nonexistent crevice between guard and tackle on the left side. Instead of trying to wrap up my legs and wrestle me down, however, the heavyweight defenders clumsily pounded the bulging pad with their padded fists and elbows. Groaning as if mortally wounded, I kept pumping my knees, moving the upright pile back, back, back for a seven-yard gain. Wearing a false face of anguish, I clutched the pad as I trudged to our huddle. They got the message: The next play might be my last.

Would you believe that my all-white tormentors never wised up to the con? They kept pounding and verbally taunting me. I kept groaning, grimacing, and running—gaining 165 yards on 25 carries. Wisconsin 14, Northwestern 6.

In the TV announcers' booth above the stands, Red Grange, the immortal "Galloping Ghost," described my performance with a mouthful of superlatives. A few days later at a football banquet in Mattoon, Illinois, he named the best running backs he had seen that year: "Johnny Karras of Illinois, Emil Sitko of Notre Dame, and Bob Teague of Wisconsin."

A couple of days after that, the Big Ten coaches—undoubtedly impressed by my numbers at Dyche Stadium—elected me, along with Johnny Karras, to the conference all-star team.

That recognition was no small factor, you can bet, in the job offer I accepted from *The Milwaukee Journal* before my graduation from Wisconsin: Staff reporter with a byline.

Are you beginning to appreciate the possible repercussions from finesse?

HI BIG GUY,

Up front—word of honor—what I am about to say is true though it may sound incredible. One ordinary day in the life of a street reporter brought an unconnected chain of events that gave me a frightening updated picture of racism.

I give you April 9, 1987—a day of revelation and infamy.

The morning headline on WINS "all-news radio" produced the first jolt. At 5:40 A.M., as I exercised on the rowing machine in my den, the anchorman said, "Superstar Dwight Gooden of the Mets, side-lined with a cocaine habit, faces probation problems in Florida . . ."

Pulling at the oars, I reacted aloud. "Geev eet to heem!" Yep. I was wishing that the normally unjust criminal justice system would make an example of a wayward brother. A black millionaire. Jealousy? Not a bit of it. In my eyes, Dwight had become a black liability. No longer the kind of dude that I wanted our kids to emulate. This was at a time when racism was rearing its ugly head with more venom spewing than I had seen since the early sixties. In recent months, before his confinement to a drug rehabilitation center in Manhattan, white and black rednecks had been dominating New York headlines. Some of the progress achieved over the past five generations was being eroded. Gooden's degredation stirred up bitter sediments. Like the wasted life of the late Len Bias, a college-basketball superman. I had lost count of the promising black youths who had taken a wrong turn down Overdose Alley. Bias had just signed an NBA contract that soon would have made him a millionaire. It was too late for me to give him the punishment he deserved; he had reinforced the myth that black people suffer irreversible brain damage at birth.

So I let Gooden have it. With both barrels. "Send his arse to the slammer," I prayed to any supernatural power who might be in the market for a soul. I had to wonder whether my attitude was proper for a black man.

14   A couple of minutes passed. I kept rowing. Pondering. Slowly, against my will, I was forced to acknowledge yet another painful intrusion of reality: There were no official guidelines for charting the maze, only a cacophony of passionate voices. I was reminded of an Arabian proverb: "By the time I grew old enough to realize that my father was right, I had a son who disagreed with me."

Forgive me. I digress. I had been lamenting Dwight Gooden's moronic plunge. There he was, on that marvelous plateau where the luckiest men alive have everything going for them. Then came his shove-it-up-the-nose dive.

Shortly before Christmas '86, I had traveled to Tampa and St. Petersburg, Florida, to cover Gooden's tribulations for *News 4 New York*. Ergo, I knew all about his latest in a zany series of confrontations with Southern cops. Dwight and his sympathizers cried, "Racist frame-up." The police cried, "Reckless driving, assault, and resisting arrest." (Think back, Adam. Which side had you believed at that time?)

Now the WINS newscaster was saying that the fabled smokeball phenom, on probation due to a plea bargain, would be subject to random drug testing over the next three years. "Failing any test could mean being sent to prison," a baseball spokesman threatened.

An irrational corner of my psyche conceived a fantasy. Suppose the white power structure agreed to let racism live or die on one roll of the dice— Gooden's case? If he stopped sucking poison up his nose and started frustrating sluggers again, the Ku Klux Klan et al. would apologize, disband, then apply for readmission to the human race. If, however, Gooden continued to believe that reality is only for people who can't handle drugs, then black stereotypes and everybody else with a nonwhite face would be obliged to return—singing and shuffling—to the kitchens and cotton fields of yesteryear; to the end of every line for good stuff; back to the back of the bus.

DEAR ADAM,

Getting back to my epiphanies of April 9 . . .

As usual, I arrived in the WNBC-TV newsroom around 6:45 A.M., fifteen minutes early. At that hour, most of Gotham was barely stirring. Only a skeleton crew of five were at their desks, laboring over the keyboards of interfacing computers, and picking the brains of strangers via telephones.

Our newsroom is on the seventh floor of a skyscraper in Rockefeller Center. I went through my daily influx of press releases, hard-luck appeals, and fan mail. One mimeographed handout startled and depressed me: An invitation to a news conference in Washington, D.C. "The Commission for Racial Justice, under the aegis of the United Church of Christ" promised to expose the sinister role that racism plays "in the location of hazardous waste sites in a disproportionate number of racial and ethnic communities throughout the United States . . ."

I sighed, shaking my head. Would there never be an end to the bizarre pranks covertly engineered by Mr. Charlie? How many miles of picketing would it take to counter that one? How many lawsuits? Damn. What cumbersome rigmaroles we had to go through ad infinitum.

Even worse, I could only guesstimate the

number of defenses I had jerry-built around my fragile ego. Was it fifty-seven or fifty-nine? Would I still have the ingenuity to cope with the next fifty-nine denials of my humanity?

I felt weary, a sigh or two from exhaustion. The weight of all the handicaps that white folks had so casually imposed on blacks and Hispanics were threatening once again to crush my spirit.

Perhaps because a Nazi war criminal was on trial in Israel, the Holocaust came to mind. Surely the depths of my anger and despair had also been suffered by helpless *Juden* in Hitler's death camps. No matter how many crackpots one managed to survive, there was always another, often more monstrous than the last.

So I rallied my beleagured variegated egos for the umpteenth time. To give in to that woe-is-me-forever mentality would mean that Mr. Charlie had won. I had to cling to my private concept of self. Not his. With whatever resources I could harness, I had to keep fighting back. It was imperative, however, to shun any weapon that would backfire.

In other words, I joined Eldridge Cleaver, H. Rap Brown, and other dropouts from the school of violent revolution. We had come to understand that even if we proved to be faster on the draw, we couldn't hope to outlast the bad guys in a shootout.

Now, armed with college degrees and marketable skills, we are fighting even harder on a different front.

DEAR ADAM,

Reading an unsigned indictment from an ex-fan that crowded morning last April gave your old man another shock.

"Mr. Teague:

"Since you put a story on the air last week portraying Brother Alton Maddox, C. Vernon Mason and other black defense attorneys as a bunch of racist fanatics, I no longer have any respect for you. Some day you are going to need the black community, but we will not be there for you."

Without the name and address of my hanging judge, I had no chance to plead not guilty. Was it my fault that, like Cyrano de Bergerac, I had "an eye to see things as they are"?

In this instance, I had been covering the trial of two black thugs, Darren Norman and Steve Bowman. They were charged with slashing the face of a white fashion model, Marla Hanson. Prior to their trial, both defendants had confessed to detectives. Furthermore, in a separate trial four months earlier, a white landlord, Steve Roth, had been convicted of hiring Bowman and Norman to perpetrate that bloody outrage. The woman had spurned Roth's invitations to Trystville.

Under those circumstances, can you imagine

how ludicrous Defense Attorney Maddox sounded in court when he argued:

(a) Roth himself had disfigured the blond model with a razor;

(b) White cops and prosecutors had framed Norman and Bowman simply because they were two blacks who happened to be at the scene of the crime?

Every TV, radio, and print newshawk in the courtroom, I knew, was wondering: "What about the victim's identification of these two dudes shortly after their arrest?"

Maddox countered by presenting another excerpt from his convoluted scenario. After describing Hanson as "a transplanted Texan," he accused her of harboring such deeply ingrained prejudices against black people that "she could not imagine a razor in the hands of a white man."

Where was the line, I wondered, that lawyers stepped over when they went beyond merely bending or stretching the truth? Did the adversary system of their profession justify such descents into sophistry?

Which explains why I began my report on the 6 P.M. news show with this on-camera commentary:

"Scarcely anyone in their right mind could argue with the reality that racism does exist in many areas of our society. In jobs and housing, in education and politics, and the criminal justice system. Does it necessarily follow, however, that all or most black defendants are therefore innocent victims of racial bias? Or is racism being misused at times to defend common criminals?"

My question was immediately answered on videotape by Roy Innis, the controversial director of the Congress of Racial Equality: "In every black-white confrontation, we are too often tempted to cry racism. Mind you, there are plenty of real situations where racism needs to be exposed and fought with everything we've got. But if we cry wolf too often, we will lose our credibility with the public."

Amen.

Of course I had deliberately tracked the man down for my report, knowing his views on that subject. He recently had lost an election for public office in a predominantly black district of Brooklyn; the majority out there didn't like his outspoken defense of Bernie Goetz. The so-called "Subway Vigilante" was currently on trial in Manhattan for wounding four black teenagers with an unlicensed .38 revolver. It had happened on a subway train after one of the punks asked Goetz to give him five dollars. Which had given Goetz the notion—later confirmed by the wounded four—that indeed they were going to rob the guy then and there.

"We need more New Yorkers like Bernie Goetz," Innis declared, amplifying our shared philosophy. "I mean the kind of people, black or white, who stand up against crime and criminals."

Black reaction to Innis's position and mine was extremely negative, but only in the less-enlightened quadrants of our community, I am pleased to say. I was reminded of the invisible tightrope that black politicians usually walk. They have to be extremely careful about acknowledging any wrong-doings by blacks, and equally reluctant to give credit to any white who just happened to be in the right.

How much more time will it take before blacks and whites start collaborating on their intertwined destinies? Never, I decided, if the shibboleths nurtured by too many members of both camps remain unchallenged.

Wrestling with those paralyzing contradictions in my mind, I came up with an excuse for Maddox's behavior. Deliberately, however, I left it out of my news report. Maddox, in a zillion legal battles, had unmasked a legion of rednecks masquerading as Christians. In the process, he had muddled his own Christian concepts. Moreover, he had forgotten his training in logic, his commitment to truth and justice. Why? Because he had seen precious little of those American ideals in the administration of justice for our people. Yes. Racism drives all of us to varying degrees of lunacy. Mr. Charlie himself is no exception.

In another segment of the controversial package that evening, C. Vernon Mason defended his colleague in a news conference. "Alton Maddox didn't invent racism. He is a victim of it."

No one who knew the man's track record could argue with that. I recalled a truly magnificent coup that Maddox and Mason had legally engineered only a few months earlier in a different case. After the infamous Howard Beach Incident of December 1986, these two black champions had accused cops and the district attorney's surrogates of a racist cover-up. Initially, I and other newshawks were skeptical. Despite our veiled criticism, however, they persisted. There was a white conspiracy, they said, to protect the mob that had attacked three black men one night, chasing one of them to his death on a busy highway.

Generally, the media had accepted the DA's explanation of his inability to prosecute more than three of the white punks involved: Most of the white witnesses regarded the mob as heroes. Which did make a regrettable kind of sense. Nearly all-white enclaves everywhere in the city had significant numbers of racists. They would intimidate anyone who even thought of taking sides with black victims.

Eventually, however, Governor Cuomo, under relentless pressure from the two black lawyers, appointed a special white prosecutor as they had demanded. Quicker than you could say "the Howard Beach Three," Prosecutor Joseph Hynes corraled a new bunch of white witnesses. A new grand jury was impressed, indicting the so-called "Dirty Dozen."

My bottom line? The trick for our side and Mr. Charlie's is to judge each black-white conundrum on the basis of the best evidence available, and to reject any argument that shorts out our logic circuits. A tricky shoal for the Good Ship Rhyme and Reason? You bet. Nevertheless, we have to try.

Some months earlier, near the beginning of the Howard Beach saga, I had made such a reasonable judgment. It led to a fistfight that I am deeply ashamed to remember. I was covering a news conference called by a coalition of a hundred-odd predominantly white labor unions. Their purpose was "to denounce racism and its ugly consequences—the white violence against innocent blacks in Howard Beach." An angry white union president thundered his indignation at the podium. His style and intensity smacked of TV evangelists.

Every reporter in the shabby old meeting hall, I presumed, had been poised to raise the logical question that I managed to blurt out first: "I understand that the emphasis here is on Howard Beach, but no one has said a word—not one of ten speakers has said a word—about that other racial attack in Jamaica, Queens: Black violence against an innocent white."

After a hushed pause of perhaps eight seconds, the master of ceremonies dismissed my objection. He explained, through clenched teeth, "That . . . was a response to a condition . . . the situation that exists. It's not for us to tell black people how they should react to the violence being inflicted upon them."

I thought, how about a 007-type license to kill?

No one applauded the white man with clenched teeth. The hundred-odd labor leaders who glared at me, however, signified their endorsement of the emcee's astonishing carte blanche.

I did not feel deflated. Everybody in that hall, including me, was walking separate but equally slippery tightropes. It was essential to my sense of integrity as a journalist—and as a concerned person—to suggest that their well-intentioned manifesto had not gone far enough in the opposite direction.

A day or two after that news conference, I was braced by one of the glaring participants. Call him Julius, a feisty little white guy in his early sixties. "You shouldn't have raised that question the other day," he whined. The two of us were shopping in a novelty store in our Upper West Side neighborhood. Although never close friends, Julius and I had known each other for several years. A former TV news technician at Channel 4, he stood five feet six or seven, weighing less than one hundred fifty pounds. "You play right into the hands of the racists when you ask a question like that," he admonished.

I wondered, how could a man whine and cackle at the same time? His voice was like sandpaper on the raw edges of my nerves. "You are entitled to your opinion, Julius," I conceded through clenched teeth. "So am I. Let's leave it at that. Please."

Julius not only ignored my request, he escalated the whine in his cackle. I swear to you, my son, I tried three or four times to walk away. I kept telling the little guy that I didn't want to discuss it.

"Get away from me, please," I growled. "Just leave me alone." I had not been that angry since the day I had filed for divorce.

Julius failed to heed the dangerous edge in my voice. Clutching my elbow, he dogged me to the other side of the store. "You've sold out," he accused, "like all the rest of 'em."

I swear again that I hadn't planned what happened next. I went berserk. Grabbing the nagging runt by the lapels of his coat, I slammed him against a wall. "Get away from me," I bellowed like a wounded bull. Julius slid to the floor, flailing at me without effect. Seizing his lapels again, I flung him through the open front door onto the sidewalk. "You made me do that," I alibied, as angry with myself as with him. I could not recall the last time that anyone had goaded me to violence. I normally took pride in my ability to walk away from loudmouths of any color, but Julius had penetrated my best defense mechanisms.

My disappointment in myself was compounded by his age and size. I was five or six years younger, half a foot taller, and forty pounds heavier. What if Julius had been five or six years younger, half a foot taller, and forty pounds heavier? Would I not have managed to curb the primitive avenger who is not the better part of me?

DEAR ADAM,

After scanning the mail on my desk that April morning, I focused on the final edition of the *Daily News*. Yep. The normal litany of disaster, crime, and gossip. The hard-boiled reporter in my psyche shrugged a shoulder. Then I read the unconsciously racist comments of baseball executive Al Campanis. My guts churned. During a nationally televised interview to salute, ironically, the fortieth anniversary of Jackie Robinson's historic debut with the 1947 Brooklyn Dodgers, Campanis had spelled out a tacit assumption among overlords of the major leagues: Black men simply "may not have the necessities." They are unfit, that is, to become field managers and front-office executives. Otherwise, he implied, they certainly would have moved up there by now. "Sorry about that," his regretful tone telegraphed to the audience, "but you can't blame us for genetics." Besides, hadn't God compensated blacks for their shortcomings? They had been given an abundance of necessities for hitting home runs and stealing bases; for scoring touchdowns, slam dunks, and knockouts.

Despite a sheepish apology that merely compounded his indiscretion, Campanis was fired by the Los Angeles Dodgers. I found minimal consolation in that. My overriding despair was summed up by Carl T. Rowan, a syndicated black columnist, in the *New York Post:*

"In his bumbling way, Jackie Robinson's former teammate blurted out what many white people in America think at every level . . . in corporate boardrooms . . . we [also] see assumptions of black inferiority in the staffing of the White House and the Reagan Administration. The cries against 'affirmative action' smell of the belief that wherever a black man gets a good job, some 'superior' white man has been cheated."

My blood pressure reached for the sky. I felt like shouting obscenities. I wanted to smash something, kill something white with my bare hands. I recalled that during my second year as a reporter at Channel 4, a handsome white newswriter had invited me to his apartment for dinner. After his wife served his third Scotch on the rocks, however, his bonhomie disappeared. Prior to my arrival at Channel 4, he said bitterly, he had been considered for promotion to full-time reporter. "You took my job, you son of a bitch," he shouted. I went for his throat.

Our wives pulled us apart before any real damage was done.

Getting back to the Al Campanis theory of genetics, I was more or less compelled to wonder about my qualifications for the executive suite. I had been in news biz twenty-four years at that point in time. Why hadn't I moved up there by now?

"Hey, wait a minute," the logician in my psyche

interrupted. "The record is clear, and you have no reason to doubt yourself. The big lie of black inferiority has been told so often over the years in so many different words that it can shake your confidence momentarily."

Yeah. Which led me to wonder: How many of us have actually mapped the minefield of racism? From Square One, when a black man leaves his sanctuary each morning, he is regarded and treated by perhaps most members of the ruling majority as an abnormality, a lower form of life. They see him as the potential perpetrator of the next violent crime to be reprised on the six o'clock news; a contaminated descendant of the African savages who invented sickle-cell anemia and probably AIDS; the primary cause of overcrowded prisons and urban blight; the most likely failure to eventually succeed as a pimp, crack dealer, or deadbeat.

Individually, we share those presumed disqualifications in their eyes. Until, that is, we scramble for opportunities to showcase the full dimensions of our complex matrix. A darker mirror image of themselves.

I can tell you from experience that trying to walk tall under the weight of such an onerous stigma, day after day for more than fifty years, is enough to drive a man to drink. To say nothing of mixing his metaphors.

DEAR ADAM,

My head trips on April 9 were interrupted by company business. I was assigned to tape an update on the previous day's top story: A mysterious gas explosion in a Bronx bodega. Six dead, twenty-nine injured.

On the scene with my two-man crew, I watched rescue workers sift through the rubble. Clearly, they were hoping against hope that they would not find what they sought. Presently, a Channel 4 colleague, John Miller, arrived with a second crew. Surprise. I couldn't imagine the assignment desk's reasoning. Barely in his thirties, Miller stood tall; as blond and good-looking as a matinee idol. Perhaps the best crime reporter on the New York tube.

After comparing notes, we decided that the desk had miscalculated. There were not enough viable story elements—interviewees, action, and suspense—to divide the coverage. Having already taped the best of a meager lot, I was the logical choice. John, a young old pro, backed off without rancor.

Later, as we rode alone in John's car from the scuzzy South Bronx to the glamour of Manhattan, our shop talk covered recent assignments. When we got around to the sensátional ongoing criminal trials, race came up. He wanted my assessment of how deeply the viper of racism was now biting into the Big Apple. His own conclusion was apparent in the matrix of a rambling question. ". . . and is it for real or just my imagination that what I've been hearing lately, at all-white parties and hanging out in gin mills, sounds like the ugly old days before Martin Luther King?"

I concurred. "I hasten to add, though, that all of us in news biz are inadvertantly feeding and goading that snake every day. I'm talking about the endless parade of black and Hispanic psychopaths on their way to jail in handcuffs. Violent punks reprising violence while on parole. White reaction, inevitably, has escalated to backlash. As if to say, 'We gave them a couple of breaks, and look at how they pay us back.'

"Since my black skin provides no protection from such violence, I've got a little backlash going on my own. Being a member of the upper middle class, I too feel twinges of anxiety when facing black or Hispanic strangers in the night. Okay, let me tell it like it is: Quite bloody often, I am so scared that I release the safety catch on the .25 automatic in my pocket. I never leave home without it." (Adam, it wasn't easy for your dad to admit those feelings privately, verbally, or in print. As sort of a black elder statesman, I believe that I must trust my guts; I must share what I perceive to be the whole truth. I am convinced, in spite of the pain, that only with the whole truth will we eventually understand and overcome.)

Back inside John Miller's car . . .

I went on to tell the young white reporter about the corollary views of Gus Heningburg. An astute political scientist, Heningburg is a public-affairs personality on Channel 4. You know, a respectable resident of the low-budget video ghetto on Sunday mornings. He had recently delivered the boldest speech that I had ever heard a black celebrity give facing a hostile audience in Harlem. "We have got to start looking at what is going on in our homes." His tone made it more of a command than a suggestion. "What has happened to the close-knit black families that used to hold our communities together? Shouldn't we admit to ourselves that we have lost control of our children? Yes, that is what I said, and that is what I meant to say. Our kids are out of control.

"Haven't you noticed, as a lot of people have, that many black parents in our inner cities are afraid of their own youngsters? To say nothing of their neighbors' children." Heningburg, a scholarly looking gray-haired giant, glared at his squirming audience. "Don't you think it is time we faced up to that? Don't we also have a responsibility to do something about it? Think of the awful consequences if we don't."

At least a part of the syndrome outlined by Heningburg, I explained to Miller, could be traced back to the civil rights advances and retreats of recent memory. In the late sixties, white guilt and sympathy began to reduce the daily output of racist bile. That was evident in virtually every American institution. Some color was added to the concept of law and order. Hallelujah and pass the black-eyed peas!

Blacks surged forward in the seventies. A new pride, bold and assertive, developed in formerly docile precincts. What no one foresaw was the scary side effect of the proverbial "loosened yoke." Brace yourself, lad. I am referring to nasty overreactions among largely disenfranchised and miserable blacks. A taste of freedom made them more impatient than ever for the feast. But many racial barriers had yet to crumble. As a consequence, in many ghettos black pride became a volatile mixture of rage and hate. By 1980 it had congealed into shtiks of dynamite.

32 As a consequence, in many white neighborhoods old racial barriers were resurrected; the remaining ones were reinforced.

We further slowed black progress by increasing our consumption of drugs—the devil's defecation in a ten-dollar plastic mini-vial.

Turning to Miller, I threw up both hands and sighed. "Man, talk about vicious circles. Each bad example on their side of the equation, and each bad example on our side, often doubled or trebeled the negatives."

The white guy behind the steering wheel gave me an Oliver Hardy double take. "Equation? Jesus, Black Arrow, what happened to the shtiks of dynamite? I mean, don't you ever stop switching your metaphors?"

My grin, I suppose, was rather awkward. "Only when telling a lie."

Miller returned my grin with minimum interest, his eyes on the swarming southbound traffic straight ahead. We were moving swiftly down the FDR Drive along the dirty gray expanse of the East River. "Uh, you've been thinking about all that stuff for some time."

Bull's-eye.

"Would you believe for over half a century?" I said with a chuckle. "Perhaps a dozen times every day." I spared young John the rest of it. The time had come to start concentrating. Before long, I would be back at the studio working with an Editek operator in the EJ (Electronic Journalism) complex on the seventh floor. How was I going to rejuxtapose the various sights and sounds on my videotape? What dramatic combination would grab the viewers, hold them spellbound for the duration of today's two-minute movie?

A deeper, quiescent level of my consciousness remained preoccupied, extending the implications of my private observations. The irony, for example, of the role that integration had played in the dissolution of the black family structure. As vigorous white enforcement of new civil rights laws opened new territory, we scattered ourselves among Mr. Charlie's folks. The cohesion we had enjoyed in our segregated slums soon vanished. Welfare allowances, something for nothing, were widely regarded as reparations, justly deserved.

Ambition waned in many families. It no longer seemed necessary to strive for higher education or better jobs. Family discipline became a thing of the past.

To me, there was a causal nexus between that part of our past and our present discontent. I thought of some relevant stories I had covered in the eighties. Like the murder of black grafitti artist Michael Stewart. After being hog-tied in the subway, he was beaten and choked by half a dozen white Transit cops. None was convicted in the trial, which reeked of racism. The late Michael Stewart, in his early twenties, was judged to have caused his own death by resisting arrest.

There was also the case of the late Eleanor Bumpurs. A certified psycho in her sixties, Mrs. Bumpurs had been reduced from a three-hundred-pound bogeywoman to a martyr with ambiguous credentials. A white cop, Officer Sullivan, had performed that legerdermain with a second shotgun blast. His first blistering serve of hot pellets had splintered the right hand of Public Enemy No. 1984, along with a large kitchen knife. Sullivan and four other white cops had legally been trying to evict a deranged deadbeat from her city-owned low-rent apartment.

From the evidence presented in court, it was quite clear that racism had played no small role in both unnecessary killings. We are talking here about megavillany.

On the other hand, if the young grafitti "artist" had not elected to flout the law by mixing painting with vandalism, wouldn't he still be alive today? Suppose his family had taught him to respect rules that were not designed to frustrate blacks.

As for Mrs. Bumpurs, her violent exit from this planet also could have been averted, by her family. Instead of canonizing the old woman, suppose they had bothered to offer help when she was alive. Why had they allowed her to live alone in a city project, totally dependent on welfare? Where were they when she lost eight or nine consecutive monthly struggles to pay the rent? Where was their compassion when they recognized, as several neighbors had, that the grossly obese and ailing Mrs. Bumpurs had lost whole departments of her mind?

No, I am not arguing that Crime A justifies Crime B. I am suggesting, however, that everybody should look closely at that inescapable linkage. I also submit that if we are as smart as we claim to be, we will stop shooting ourselves in the foot.

Let me remind you that in the Elysian enclaves of American dreams come true, there is a semi-religious reverence for the democratic dynamics of negotiation, give and take, telling it like it is, and owning up to one's mistakes.

It had dawned on many honest reporters, long before my time, that, regardless of what the signs read, there is no such thing as a one-way street. In the multiracial experiment called America, every imperfect participant must compete under the same set of rules. Only then can we expect to have peace with honor. Only then can we reject the divisive fiction that compromise is a four-letter word for losers. Without compromise, without mutual respect, there can be no trust. Good-bye, brotherhood of man.

36

MY SON, MY SON,

What a mitzvah it is having you as the only living extension of myself into tomorrow.

Having just wound up our first double date at my table, I am inspired. For the moment, forget the verbal firecrackers I've been setting off in recent letters. Right now I want to talk about love. Mine for you.

I am very proud of the way you handle yourself. Not only in the presence of Lady Jan and Sasha tonight. You seem to have a thoughtful approach to life on every front, modestly succeeding here and there.

During dinner, I felt constrained to lift the curtain that conceals my vulnerability. There are gooey marshmallows at the core of my manly affection. Freudian stuff. In your eyes, I could have been treating you like a pup in front of your girlfriend. Whew! That was close. Even the best fathers have to dodge bullets like that all their lives.

Anyway, what I'm getting at is how proud I am that you have grown strong and willful. Man enough to do it your way. As a brash youth of twenty-one, I had overruled my old man, in similar respects. I have never regretted my choices.

Tonight I might sell my body to the Ku Klux Klan if that would guarantee for you, my son, the kind of happiness, success, and fulfillment that I have known. Can you imagine any father wanting anything less for his child?

Within earshot of Jan and Sasha, I also felt constrained to announce my acceptance of the dwindling contacts between father and man-son. "Leaving the nest," Freud called it. Lady Jan calls it "one of the primitive games that very few guys can resist. You have to prove to whom it may concern that you are the better man."

She got that right. Every one of us would like to go one-up some day on the tough old rascal who has outsmarted and outeverythinged us for all those bloody years.

Being a forty-two-year-old psychoanalyst in training, Lady Jan knows her way around human frailties.

What especially pleases me about you, Adam, is the promising blend of stuff that you have and have not done. Largely on your own. In this context, I probably sound like a Jewish mother. Why not? That, in my learned opinion, is what moms and dads have in common almost everywhere. With my Channel 4 colleagues, I actually hear myself saying, "My son Adam who is this much taller than me . . ." With a Yiddish accent yet. In New York—where the Jewish population is larger than it is in Israel—everybody becomes a little kosher.

My Adam. What a maven he's going to be.

Only twenty-one years old and already he knows you shouldn't hang a millstone of dope around your neck. He is smart enough already to do sex without making somebody a grandpa before my time.

Though regularly exposed to the painful absurdities of racism, your central core of self remains intact; your sense of humor, irrepressible. There is a look in your gentle but suspicious brown eyes that quietly says with conviction: "I'm playing to win."

I find it fun being a rarely used safety net for a bloke like that.

Oh, I admit to having been deeply disappointed when you opted to postpone college indefinitely. What I'm saying here is, you have won me over. By performance. Though four years shy of a collegiate veneer, you have learned some of the nitty-gritty that makes life manageable. While working part-time in your adopted uncle's bakery and waiting on tables in Sasha and Company's restaurant, you have also found time to continue your education part-time—at NYU, the Art Students League, and the New School. Significantly, you have only come to me for help with paying for guitar lessons. By your own sweat and ingenuity, you also have managed to study TV photography, videotape editing, and film animation. And I have seen you performing song and comedy bits with other unpaid, unseasoned hams.

Somewhere in that self-generated maelstrom,

you will find the rest of yourself. And a career
Somewhere, I suspect, in show biz.

Getting back to our double date with Lady Jan
and Sasha . . .

What a long way you and I have traveled together with women since Yvonne. Remember our
first skiing weekend in the Berkshires in 1975? You
were nine years old. The beautiful female with us
was making suitable overtures for your approval.
Having driven up to the Bay State on a Friday
night, we were staying in a rambling old wooden
farmhouse with the Prisendorffs and their two ram-
bunctious boys who were around your age.

Through some pretext, you isolated Yvonne the
following morning. A sneaky little wise guy, you
more or less ordered her to get lost.

Yvonne came to me in tears. Oddly, she
blamed herself for having failed to win you over;
she already had been resigned to settling for
something less than your affection. Which brought
you and me to the Oedipal showdown that I had
dreaded. Yvonne was the second usurper you had
tolerated grudgingly since your mother and I tore
up our contract in the spring of '74.

"Come over here, Tiger," I said sternly. "It's
time we had a little talk in private. . . . So you did a
big number on Yvonne. You don't have to answer. I
already know what's on your mind. If she disap-
pears, as Alice did, you might have a shot at re-
establishing the best of all possible worlds; that is,
having not one but two obedient subjects in your
kingdom all week long. Forget about it. That is

never going to happen, see? For reasons that you are too young to understand, there is nothing between your mother and me anymore. Except alimony: The screwing a man gets for the screwing he got. You know enough to understand that. So we might as well straighten this out once and for all."

I took a deep breath, consulting my guts, recalling no relevant counsel from Dr. Spock. "I think you appreciate by now that female critters are very important to your daddy. If you force me to make a choice . . . if you take it that far, Tiger . . . guess how I am going to choose?"

Nothing more was ever said about that until now.

Had I been bluffing back there in the Berkshires? Nope. Long before that time in my life, I had become thoroughly disenchanted with the permissive school of parenting. Dr. Spock, I deduced, had never been challenged by the likes of my Adam-Smasher.

"Don't spank him," your mother would plead against almost any hint of discipline. "You'll warp his little personality."

"Better me than the warden," I argued back. "This boy has got to understand that he lives in a world with other people. He can't always have it his way. Sure, it's a jungle out there. But dammit to hell, there are rules." Whack, whack, whack went my rolled-up copy of the Sunday *Times* magazine against your bottom.

Vivid memories of stiffer punishment from my

father's heavy leather belt restrained my hand; I always made a conscious effort to keep your spankings more symbolic than physical. Disapproval, I believed, was the real message. I am not saying it hurt me more than you. Nor am I apologizing. I was driven to inflict penalties by envisioning traumatic psychodramas of your future. I could see you as you might have turned out without some parental punishments when deserved. I didn't want my boy to become a self-centered, arrogant punk. Without the twenty-odd spankings I gave you before our family fell apart, I believe even now that you might have evolved into an obnoxious character. Unreliable and disrespectful. Without the converse of those traits, you would not have received the nurturing and mentoring that everybody needs from a succession of human support systems.

Happily, I think my expertise with rolled-up copies of the Sunday *Times* magazine has paid off handsomely.

At the same time, however, I honestly feel entitled to very little credit for the hard-working dude you've become. To my way of thinking, you benefited most from the dedication of several private-school teachers, black and white; they really cared about you and your future. Seeing your negative potential to be a wounded refugee from a shattered sanctuary, they understood. You could have become a real pain in the arse, but they wouldn't let you.

Though most of your former mentors at City and Country School have vanished for one reason or another, I sent a small donation to the scholarship fund not long ago: A token of my gratitude to those professional surrogates. They had been there to take up the awesome slack that had been left by your fugitive father.

DEAR ADAM,

Another embarrassing sign of our dispiriting decline was exposed today by the media. "A majority of parents with children in New York City's public schools," the *Daily News* snitched, "have not met their kids' teachers; nor do they know if their child does homework."

Citing a 1987 survey conducted by the school principals' union, the report charged that only 36 percent of the six hundred parents who responded in a telephone poll had bothered to introduce themselves to teachers or participate in school affairs. Only 27 percent had made an effort to assist their children with homework.

Hang on, Tiger. The worst is yet to come.

Both the *Daily News* and the principals were too discreet to break those statistics down along racial lines. Had they done so, I suspect, black and Hispanic parents would have fallen well below those dismal norms.

"Those numbers are disturbing," understated Ted Elsberg, president of the Council of Supervisors and Administrators. "If school performance is to improve, parents will have to be more involved."

Disturbing? Hell, I would say catastrophic. As in uneducated, unemployed, and unworthy of respect. I mean, we are talking here about despised, downtrodden minorities who give lip service to civilized aspirations.

Compounding parental shame, the survey further showed that as their youngsters advanced through the system—learning little and caring less—moms and dads gave diminishing attention to schoolwork. At the high school level, only 7 percent seemed to be even minimally involved.

It avails us naught to fall back on the survey's mitigating footnote: "The results of the poll indicated that an increase in single-parent households, a significant number of homes where the parents do not speak English, and a growing percentage of homes with two working parents all have contributed to cutting down parental involvement."

True, those circumstances represent onerous impediments for black and Hispanic parents at the sorry end of the socioeconomic totem pole. However, instead of throwing up both hands in despair, I say we should try harder.

Consider the approach being taken these days by Mamie Johnson, principal of Public School 146 in East Harlem. Although many families in that discouraging neighborhood live under constant stress, Johnson has enlisted them in a successful working partnership. In six years, the number of kids reading at grade level has climbed from 33 percent to 65 percent. Who says poor minority kids can't learn?

"These kids are the future," Johnson declared at a recent gathering of the Parents and Teachers Association. "We want parents to know what our expectations are and how they can help."

Here are four of the parental guidelines she promulgates:

Provide a quiet study corner at home.

Monitor your children's homework.

Set aside regular time periods when your whole family engages in silent reading.

You are required to come to the school to pick up your kids' report cards.

Under the aegis of the redoubtable Mamie Johnson, P.S. 146 also operates, informally, as a crisis-prevention center. Which means that she and her teachers counsel disadvantaged families under stress and refer them to appropriate social-service agencies.

The superintendent of that improving East Harlem school district, Carlos Medina—publicly praising the principal's bold initiatives—announced plans for a district-wide crisis center. "If we help our parents cope with stress," he explained, "their children will come to school in a better frame of mind for learning."

We are talking here about self-help; not protest marches, sit-ins, prayers, or petitions.

Mamie Johnson's vision, inspiration, and accomplishments are all the more pertinent when you factor in her humble background: The eldest of ten children in a poor family in East Harlem, she had spent part of her childhood in a rundown tenement just up the street from P.S. 146. After finishing high school, she worked days for seven years to help put food on the table and pay the rent while attending night school to become a teacher. Since then she has earned two master's degrees and is now working on her Ph.D.

Meanwhile—recognizing how far her black and Hispanic students have to go to catch up with their white and Asian competitors out there—Mamie Johnson makes house calls on Sundays.

DEAR ADAM,

Recalling the trials and errors of your childhood in a previous letter has automatically dredged up some of mine. For loaded comparisons, naturally. Mine was a different era, of course, with options to match. An embarrassing number of years elapsed before my perceptions were finally in synch with reality. As in, "So that's how it is in this nuthouse. Dammit."

I especially want to zero in here on black babble. That is the stuff that often triggers our knee-jerk reflex in the wrong direction, preventing effective dealing with the Mr. Charlie Problem. Consider what might happen if we declared a moratorium on pointing fingers and calling names. That would give us time to make better use of our energy. Like reviving mass production of old-fashioned true grit and peer pressure, in tandem with modern finesse, in all of our black communities.

In the separate unequal housing sprawls of the late thirties and early forties, we knew we had to stick together to survive. Mr. Charlie's overreaction to black punks in those days was truly Draconian. And being innocent was no defense. In that climate, our parents taught us that being poor was no excuse for slovenly manners, dirty clothes, or petty crimes like shoplifting. On the contrary, being poor was an incentive to work like hell in school and part-time jobs. Which is precisely how many of us got our act together and took it on the road.

Parents had not been alone in enforcing that concept of black solidarity. In every neighborhood where my folks paid rent, you could see and hear it everywhere. Unlike black families today—isolated fragments full of pain—we recognized one another as wounded parts of ourselves. Being good neighbors meant looking out for one another's children. Kids were required to obey all respectable adults in the community. Almost every utterance that we addressed to our sovereigns was prefaced by "Sir" or "Ma'am." Violators of those rigid protocols could expect swift punishment when reported to either parent. Yes, nearly all of us lived with two parents. In retrospect, we had a sprawling black conspiracy that really worked.

At school—segregated or not—an angry teacher would send me home with a handwritten copy of my conviction. Regardless of how cleverly this guilty defendant might plead, the Mom and Pop Jury was always just. Whack, whack, whack.

Our common enemy back then was Mr. Charlie. Today, however, in many situations that I have witnessed, that is not the whole truth. In the immortal words of Pogo, the sage of Okefenokee Swamp, "We have met the enemy and he is us."

Too many black parents are now predisposed to throw out any charge against their sons and daughters if brought by whites. "They be prejudice [sic] against Bubba just because he black. My child don't be bringing no gun to school." As if to say fingerprints lie.

Under the guise of "standing up to Whitey," those ostrich-headed parents contribute to the rise of public enemies among students. Why is it so difficult for so many of them to grasp the logical consequences of that my-child-is-never-guilty "sindrome"? Which inflicts heavier casualties among our disadvantaged youth than among those who maintain the disadvantages.

Conversely, look at the upbeat results of the peer pressure of my boyhood. Very few of my playmates committed felonies and went to jail. A lesser number dared to experiment with drugs. Only three chose the neighborhood racketeer as their role model. Only one went the way of all pimps.

Our moral majority studied hard to keep up our grades. Failing any subject could result in house arrest plus hard labor over algebra problems. In my house, Adam, your wily grandparents kept me up to speed with coded threats: "Do you think that breaking a rule we've laid down is worth giving up your allowance for?" And, "If you quit the football team, wouldn't you have more time to work on your geometry?"

Under duress of that magnitude, after flunking Geometry 10B at Milwaukee Lincoln High School, I buckled down. No more failures through the remainder of high school and four years at the University of Wisconsin. My B-plus average and football skills paid off in a college scholarship.

Boys and girls of my generation were required to handle certain chores around the house: washing dishes, mopping floors, taking out garbage—onerous disruptions of playtime. We also went to menial jobs after school. I worked as a janitor in a women's shoe store, washed dishes in a Walgreen's drugstore, and typed the official correspondence for an Episcopalian Church in a white neighborhood.

Under strict instructions from the ultimate authorities in our homes, we learned to live within budgets. Which meant saving a fraction of our earnings to cushion the inevitable fall upon harder times.

Rarely did one of us kids miss a ten P.M. curfew. When we fooled around at drive-in movies and lovers' lanes, the boys took sensible precautions or the girls said no. Having a baby out of wedlock had not been deemed the status symbol it is today in several scurvy housing projects that I have covered.

Adults in my growing-up years also taught us to be ashamed of "going on relief." Kids in the upper echelon of the underclass would tease playmates whose families accepted handouts from the government. How much progress can blacks expect tomorrow if so many of our families give the impression of being content in their second and third generations on relief?

Never mind that you think some blue-eyed devil made them do it. It is not Mr. Charlie's sexual prowess that accounts for all those illegitimate babies whose mothers are welfare dependents. I have overheard a number of single moms boast of cheating Mr. Charlie out of a few thousand more welfare dollars than legally allowed. He loses, we win, right?

Yeah, if you like Pyrrhic victories.

Wouldn't it be smarter, if you were bent on cheating the system, to do it with a flourish, Sheldon Weinberg—style? Recently, at the health clinic they owned in one of the poorest black neighborhoods in Brooklyn, Weinberg and his yuppie sons Jay and Arnold were busted. The charge: Stealing over thirteen million federal tax dollars from Medicaid. (Of course they had finished college first; otherwise, they couldn't have engineered such a scam.) For several years, the DA said, the Weinbergs had programmed the clinic's computer to routinely cough up some twelve thousand phony Medicaid claims each month. If convicted, chances are the Weinbergs—still respected in most upper-class circles of this society—will serve little time behind bars. I would say considerably less time than the typical welfare chisler and the mugger who stomps an old Medicaid patient for fifteen bucks.

Yes, I know the astronomical arithmetic of black unemployment. I am painfully aware of the wide, wide gap between white income and black ends that never meet.

However, I am the sum total of all my moments, especially those with my dad. Though permanently handicapped with a fifth-grade education, he would swear with pride: "I wouldn't be caught dead on relief. If you want to be somebody, you got to work."

Lately, in the eighties, I have heard echoes of my dad among proud working blacks. Your late uncle Julian usually summed it up in one sentence: "Even if you win the welfare rat race, you're still a rat."

Amen. And the winner will never have anywhere to go except into another rathole.

My playmates and I learned about racial injustice from direct experience—the kind no longer tolerated on a massive scale even in the Deep South. With parental guidance, as advised in all civilized societies, we soon understood that each of our crimes and achievements could lower or raise the barometers of bigotry. You can't imagine how many times black monitors in every ghetto advised their rude and violent cousins to cool it. "What you're doing is going to make things worse for the rest of us."

In many black neighborhoods today, to even suggest, sotto voce, that the anti—life-styles of urban terrorists serve to reinforce unflattering stereotypes is a no-no, akin to treason.

Your generation, my son, may see the back-off-and-buckle-down approach as knuckling under. Call it whatever you like. In my judgment, what ought to count most is results.

Case in point: A recent government study of minority college students showed that "many universities found that the assimilation of significant numbers of minorities into campus life could be somewhat disruptive." You can imagine the horrible incidents glossed over by those academic euphemisms.

I don't care what the Bible promises or what the Bill of Rights guarantees. We had better start facing the enemies among us without flinching. By that I mean we must encourage and assist our cousins to stop justifying Mr. Charlie's favorite put-down: "What did I tell you? All they want is a welfare check, loose shoes, and a warm place to make babies."

Am I excusing his nasty attitude? Don't ask irrelevant questions. I am trying to recalibrate the alarm systems in our ghettos that are triggered too often by the wrong signals. In other words, if we believe in reason, we ought to be pondering more about what we can do to help ourselves in the long run; at present, we are squandering too much time on the logistics of setting up picket lines to inconvenience somebody white, temporarily.

LISTEN UP
TIGER,

This is important. As I scribble these blandishments in New York about a stand-up dude in Paterson, New Jersey, a pedigreed Hollywood screenwriter elsewhere is creating a movie about President Reagan's favorite hard-nosed high school principal. Yep. The legendary Joe Clark, appearing this week on the cover of *Time* magazine. Patroling the corridors with a bullhorn and a baseball bat, Clark has turned a blackboard jungle into a learning tree. The problems he faced had not been foisted upon him by white folks. He didn't beg whites to solve it.

I tell you this in the unabashed hope that my son will not travel with the misguided black pack— which always passes blame, never countenances shame, and wouldn't dream of looking inward instead of calling names.

A couple of weeks ago, I covered a skirmish in Clark's long-running feud with Paterson's Board of Education and Fire Department. Joe had gone too far, they charged in Superior Court, when he expelled 60 young thugs from East Side High on the grounds that their disruptive behavior was making it impossible for the other 2,940 students to concentrate on their studies, and when he padlocked several fire exits to halt the daily invasion of drug dealers, muggers, and other disgusting forms of life in the guise of slender black and Hispanic males.

Students, parents, and everybody else with a modicum of common sense stood up and saluted the former drill sergeant. His bureaucratic adversaries stubbornly ignored the relevant facts: The school board had failed to provide adequate security personnel at East Side High; and even in the worst scenario, the building could have been evacuated swiftly, as demonstrated in bullhorn-orchestrated fire drills.

Happily, Clark's successes were praised by the establishment—including President Reagan and Secretary of Education William Bennett. "If Paterson, New Jersey, can't appreciate this dedicated educator," a Reagan aide told the media, "we will give him a job here in the White House."

All of which, in my judgment, translated into a very clear signal to black folks: When you make an honest effort to clean up your own mess, you will suddenly discover allies who had once appeared to be your oppressors.

As for Clark's tactics—expelling those hooligans "without due process," said black and white nitwits on the school board—I say civilized societies have long accepted the principle that extraordinary circumstances may call for unorthodox countermeasures. By the time a phalanx of mealy-mouthed lawyers finished futzing around with due process, those garbage heads in the classrooms could have torn down East Side High.

How do you suppose the money changers in the temple would have reacted if Jesus had served them with a temporary restraining order instead of wading among the louts and flailing away with a whip?

Prime Minister Churchill's bold departure from conventional compassion probably saved Great Britain. On his orders, wounded soldiers were the last to be evacuated from the beaches of Dunkirk; top priority was given instead to able-bodied Tommys so sorely needed to defend the realm. Sir Winston also gave orders that, in the event of a Nazi invasion, Britain's beaches should be sprayed with poison gas—a blatant violation of the Geneva Convention. He further decreed that the R.A.F. should pound civilian targets in German cities, convinced in his brilliant mind that terror bombardment was essential to breaking the will of Hitler's silent majority.

Like Churchill, Joe Clark understands that when a decent chap is challenged by unspeakable, uncompromising ugliness, he does not hire the Marquis of Queensbury as a consultant.

My admiration for this right-stuff hero was concretely expressed the other day by the On-Line Software Corporation of Fort Lee, New Jersey: A million-dollar gift to East Side High—$100,000 a year for the next ten years to assist Clark's college-bound seniors. Wisely, the benefactor stipulated that the scholarship ante would be withdrawn if the fuddy-duddy school board carried out its threat to suspend or sack the tough guy who speaks with an amplified voice and carries a big Louisville Slugger. A case of justified black male, in my opinion.

"We felt strongly," a Software honcho explained out loud, "that the job was being done at East Side High under the leadership of Joe Clark. . . . We are trying to create a focus on what the important issues are. Let's get down to what Mr. Clark has done here, and the good he's done, and let's create that across the nation."

Amen.

Like your dad, Joe Clark believes that government handouts constitute the most damaging assault on black pride and dignity since the founding of the Ku Klux Klan. At the moment, the Feds are running fifty-nine major welfare scams at a cost of over a hundred billion dollars a year. Rather than rescuing minority families from poverty, however, this cradle-to-grave safety net has proved to be a pernicious trap. To paraphrase President Reagan, the government launched a war on poverty some years ago, and poverty won.

We still could effect a dramatic reversal by spending only a fraction of the current welfare budget; that is, if the money went instead to more programs that trained disadvantaged folks for specific occupations, required them to work, and provided affordable day-care centers for their children.

At the same time, at no additional cost, we have to do something drastic about the image being projected by far too many of our youngsters—rude, crude, and lacking in motivation to excel in school. To tell it like it is, far too many black kids give the impression that they have been shortchanged genetically: Real big thighs, as Jimmy the Greek once observed, implying real small brains.

It behooves us, then, to teach our kids at home the pragmatic rewards they could derive from the Paterson principal's principles: study, discipline, respect, courtesy, self-reliance, reliability, cooperation, and sweat.

Without those characterological building blocks, our kids will have no chance at all to catch up, keep up, or grow up.

DEAR ADAM,

Belatedly it occurs to me that there is a definitive phrase for the self-affliction that reduces so many of our kinfolks to sitcom caricatures: Tunnel Vision.

In Lady Jan's lexicon of abnormal psychology, TV is "an extremely narrow point of view that corrupts the rest of reality."

Like the apochryphal Rabbi Singleshtik. Speaking at the grand reopening of a renovated zoo, his topic was "The Elephant and the Jewish Problem." At a neighborhood breakfast for Good Samaritans, he explained "Scrambled Eggs and the Jewish Problem."

I confess to have chuckled over jokes like that. Yesterday, however, I didn't find it funny when a real TV personality telephoned me in the newsroom. He left me speechless.

"My name is Johnson," he began quite soberly. "Trina Johnson's father."

Instantly, I recalled the murder of an eighteen-year-old black waitress at a McDonald's restaurant in the Bronx a few days earlier. "Yes, Mr. Johnson. I covered the arrest of the two [Hispanic] guys accused of that horrible crime. What can I do for you?"

He wanted to appear on Channel 4. "I can bring out the facts about McDonald's negligence. They know that that restaurant is in a real bad neighborhood. There's crack all over that area. They should have had bulletproof glass in there to protect the employees from stickups. I don't want to see somebody else lose their daughter like I did. Her death will be in vain unless you help me to get that message across . . ."

Measuring the hard line he was taking, I sensed that it would be futile to try to talk him out of it. "Mr. Johnson," I said, making the attempt anyway, "I can understand the kind of anguish you're going through. I'm a father myself. And I know that if anything happened to my Adam . . . I would be devastated. In all honesty, however, I have to tell you this. I know a lot of places in the city where people have been killed during stickups. Supermarkets, banks, and restaurants. You name it. Yet to this day they have not installed bulletproof partitions."

"But don't you see," he interrupted, "that many other lives could be saved?"

I counted to three. "Mr. Johnson, I appreciate what you're saying. But I don't think putting bulletproof glass around the city is the answer."

"Oh, excuse me," he apologized sarcastically. "I thought you were a brother. Now I see that you're a white boy."

DEAR ADAM,

Knowing how busy and preoccupied you are, I assume that you did not see my story on the six P.M. news this evening. It was a classic case of a reporter coming that close to crying racism on the air out of context. I must keep reminding myself that white folks are not one-dimensional creatures either. Racism is neither their sole motivation nor their only imperfection.

In a white middle-class neighborhood in Queens, angry residents had set fire to a vacant house. The city welfare agency had just rented it for conversion within a month to a "group home for boarder babies." Ninety percent black and Hispanic infants. Their mothers were either junkies, hookers, or just plain ignorant girls who had never learned to say no.

Would you regard torching that house as a transparent case of racism?

I thought so at first, prejudiced no doubt by an adage from my childhood: If it walks like a duck, swims like a duck, and quacks like a duck, chances are it ain't Bugs Bunny.

Luckily, despite my broad jump to a wrong conclusion, I could not turn off my trained reporter's ear. As the suspected bigots told their side of the story on-camera, my third ear did not detect evidence of sham. Gradually, I discerned, these muddle-headed blokes were rather in synch with the human condition.

"The whole thing we're worried about," said an uptight mother of three, "is dope addicts. I love babies. But those junkie mothers are going to come here to see them. The first thing you know, you'll be afraid to even leave your house anymore."

What further helped to turn that story around for me was a revelation dutifully volunteered by a flack for the welfare agency. Last fall, she said, the Jewish Child Care Association, a private nonprofit entity, had taken steps to buy that same vacant house. The plan was to convert it to "a group home for Jewish adolescents with troubled backgrounds."

The response from the same neighbors: "No way. Not in our backyard." They envisioned themselves being swamped and intimidated by an endless procession of spaced-out freaks. Facing formidable opposition, including threats, the Jewish buyers backed out of the deal. "Trouble like that," a rabbi said, "we can do without."

Mayor Koch paid a visit to ground zero after the torching. Neighborhood opposition, he declared philosophically, would have been almost equally negative over a proposed jail, a methadone clinic, or a shelter for bag ladies. "From the poorest poor to the richest rich, nobody wants to do their part. They all say, 'Yes, we need it. Yes, we care about the homeless and the needy. But for God's sake build it over there. Not here!'"

Mr. Sarcasm himself, on the fringe of the mayor's sidewalk news conference, overrode Hizzoner with a challenge: "Why don't you put one on your block?"

Now, there was a white brother whom I could relate to; I didn't want the damn thing in my neighborhood either.

HI ADAM,

There is something else you ought to know about my "reporter's ear." Listening with it over the years has been extremely valuable in a variety of contexts. No civilized man, I believe, can afford to be without one.

Civilization can only flourish, the anthropologists say, if there are some fundamental agreements, enforceable contracts among most individuals and tribes. As we compete for pieces of the proverbial pie, we can minimize the misunderstandings that divide us by listening with that third ear. The result can mean less friction, suspicion, hate, and violence.

An attainable red-white-black-and-true-blue America?

Maybe. We have nothing to lose, however, by going for it.

History tells me that in every age, progress came when daring men and women broke away from the herd and concretized a better way of doing things.

The pivotal factor that caused my third ear to plug into yet another amplifier, and thus extend its range, may have little relevance for you at the moment, son. Like your old man thirty-odd years back yonder, you are enjoying the grand tour in the wonderful world of making whoopee. For me, where I am now—bonded with one female out of wedlock—feels exactly right at this stage of my life. I hate to think of what I might have missed without the love, respect, and understanding of Lady Jan. You have seen us together. You know how it is. We are as one-on-one as any wounded survivors of the heterosexual wars could dare to risk.

In our seventh year as a couple—with separate apartments in the same high-rise—we are united in our determination to remain that far apart. Jan usually spends five nights a week in my larger apartment. Hey, if it ain't broke, don't fix it.

I am reminded of her hard-line response at the wedding of friends when a married female among the guests confronted us. "After all these years of going together, are you two at least thinking about matrimony?"

With a Garboesque smile, my lady said firmly, "No, thanks. We both prefer sex to violence."

On cue, I reprised a malicious punchline that I had heard at the groom's bachelor party. "I'll say one thing for marriage. You never know what sex is until you get married. Then it's too late."

I don't think I have mentioned the two unsworn husbands she had lived with, one at a time of course, several years earlier. The first chap proved to be a cocaine addict. The second was an uncertified psychopath at large.

Okay, so she wound up with schizophrenic me. My madness is offset, in Lady Jan's estimation, by redeeming ambiguities: I am utterly faithful to her, and I love to cook.

It is my hope, Adam, that you eventually will segue to your dad's happy conclusion: Life is hugely satisfying when you and one lady in particular can get it on and keep it together. I say that in light of mixed experience—one glad-I-had-it marriage, a bitter divorce, two out-of-court palimony settlements, and a princely amount of freelancing in between. Ah, yes. Fun, excitement, and despair. The stuff that soap operas are made of.

You understand, then, the deterrents that prevent us from tying any kind of noose. Significantly, our arrangement is openly envied by at least one partner in every couple we know.

Being separated on Mondays and Tuesdays imbues Wednesday nights with the magic of paradise regained. We are thus more appreciative of what we mean to each other, and we show it. Besides, we have seen too many loving couples quickly evolve into unromantic adversaries after making promises at the altar that scarcely any human beings could possibly keep.

Without such vows between us, Lady Jan and I do not require each other to fit into an uncomfortable, artificial mold. We simply do what works for us. Among other benefits, we provide each other with a refuge from all the madness out there. Since neither of us is legally bound to hang in there no matter what, we play the old Eastern Airlines game, winning our wings every day.

Being happy with Jan and anxious to keep soaring in the same orbit, I have learned to listen to her with my third ear. Otherwise, I certainly would miss what she means in her complicated heart on some occasions. Now and then she says something, as I am prone to do, that at first sounds like gibberish.

Fortunately, I plugged in that extra amplifier just a few months into our relationship in '81. By that time Jan—the psychiatric social worker aiming to become a psychoanalyst—had adjusted her own third ear. She could hear the seven or eight dudes so often at war inside me. Also, she could hear the better man that I am always trying to become.

During a party last June in someone else's honor, I boasted to friends that Lady Jan and I were modestly observing our sixth anniversary as a couple that very night. "How great has it been? You won't believe how great," I crowed. "In all that time, I honestly can remember only three arguments that amounted to any serious threat to our relationship. One involved a cat that I was allergic to; the others were so undramatic that the details are fuzzy now. Oh, yeah, she dumped that cat."

There was a skeptical chorus of challenges. "Let's hear what Lady Jan has to say about all that," one soprano trilled obligato.

Without blushing or batting a blue eye, Lady Jan—joining us when summoned—set the record straight. "There were eight arguments. I remember eight." No reprimand, no explanation or accusation. Just the facts as she recalled them.

Before the chorus of infidels could start gloating aloud, they were stopped, with mouths agape, by a jealous contralto's aria. "Wait a minute. Eight hassles in six years? That works out to something like one-point-three per year."

The ensuing respectful silence was my reward. Everybody was running mental checks on their own relationships.

"Okay. One-point-three per year," I echoed— voice cool, smile urbane. "I am not going to argue with those numbers."

DEAR ADAM,

I tried to reach you on the phone late yesterday. Your loss. I wanted to invite you over for dinner and a TV rerun of *The Sea Hawk*—one of the great old Errol Flynn swashbucklers. We once enjoyed it together on the home screen long ago between episodes of *The Electric Company* and *Sesame Street.*

Watching it all alone last night, I was struck by one scene in particular. It depicted sort of a distant parallel to some current definitions of racism.

Flynn, as Captain Thorpe, commanded the English privateer *Albatross* in the late sixteenth century. After attacking and capturing a Spanish galleon, he freed dozens of English galley slaves who had been chained for life to the oars in the bowels of the ship. Rich plunder from the New World was transferred to the *Albatross* as the galleon slowly sank in the English Channel. Later, aboard the victorious vessel, the captive leading lady (Brenda Marshall) accused Captain Thorpe of being a thief.

"Tell me, Donna Maria," the captain countered slyly, "is a thief an Englishman who steals?"

"Of course not," the aristocratic lady said icily. "It's anyone who steals."

"I see. By the way, I've been admiring some of

the gold bracelets we found in your jewelry case. Aztec, isn't it? I wonder how those Indians were persuaded to part with it."

The chagrined Donna Maria found it difficult to flounce from the deck with dignity. Her skirts had been snagged on her own petard.

Now, plumping for accuracy in language and labels, let us consider these pertinent questions in the twentieth century:

1. Is a racist a white person who resents rowdy, disruptive behavior and foul language at public gatherings?

2. Are you a racist if you hate the relentless thunder of bongo drums while you are trying to sleep?

3. Am I a racist because I get hot under the collar at the sight of subway riders smoking cigarettes or pot in blatant defiance of the law and common courtesy?

4. Are racists the only subway passengers whose sensibilities are offended by sleeping drunks stretched out full-length, thus depriving four or five other straphangers of their right to sit?

5. Are only racist ears annoyed by oversized radio "blasters" played at full volume in public places?

6. How should I feel about the obnoxious neighbors who treat the sidewalk in front of my apartment house as a hangout, a place to dump empty beer cans and other garbage?

7. Am I anti–affirmative action when I scowl at certain bank tellers and civil servants who are so

engrossed in kidding around that they fail to take care of business expeditiously?

8. What attitude should one adopt when reading about roving wolfpacks snatching gold chains and purses after rock concerts?

9. Are racists the only citizens who reject the notion that poverty is an excuse for beating up smaller kids who refuse to surrender their leather jackets or their skateboards?

10. Are you against racial integration if you don't wish to work around, live near, or socialize with loutish individuals who rarely show respect for themselves, even less for others?

Which brings me back, one more time, to what is going on in too many black households these days. It is embarrassingly apparent that manners and morals have been purged from the family curriculum. How else could I explain the following story in a recent edition of the *New York Post*?

> 29 HELD IN WOLFPACK TERROR
>
> Bands of marauding black teen-agers roamed through Central Park and subways in wolfpacks yesterday on a rampage of robbery and terror. About 100 black youths, shouting "Howard Beach, Howard Beach . . ."

Did their parents know where they were, or care? What had they been teaching their youngsters, and failing to teach?

As your uncle Julian was fond of lecturing,

"Show me a delinquent child, I'll show you a delinquent parent."

Without parental monitors to back them up, public school teachers in several largely minority districts are being intimidated by X-rated punks. Having little or no interest in the three R's, they disrupt the learning process for classmates.

So what happens to that surly lot after dropping out of school or being expelled?

They blame their failure to land a good job on you-know-what.

DEAR ADAM,

I am not alone in my madness. Have just discovered a charming black middle-aged neighbor—a City University factotum living five floors below my two-bedroom asylum. His loony tunes echo my own. Call him Reno.

On the elevator this morning as we set off for work, Reno focused two bleary eyeballs on me. Had I also been kept awake, he asked, by the free bongo concert presented last night on the grungy side of our street?

"Uh-hunh. I had to restrain my lady around midnight. She had picked up my gun and opened a window."

Reno chuckled. Then, in a gravelly lisp à la Bogart, he crooned:

> "You must remember this
> some dudes are worse than piss
> and junkies always cry
> No matter what the liberals say
> as crime goes high
> And when they bother you
> it's not uncouth to sue
> or say that they're a pill
> And who could blame you
> if you did go out and kill"

Bravo, Reno. Shucks, not only one of us, he was one of me. My applause was discreet but sincere.

Accepting my admiration at its happy-face value, he formally introduced himself, then expanded. "This has been going on over there, off and on, for years, you know."

I nodded.

Reno beamed at my sagacity. "Right. They can't seem to get it into their heads that I would rather sleep in the still of the night than listen to 'La Bamba.'" He sighed, a sound that resonated with my weariness. We left the elevator in the lobby.

"I have run out of patience with them," my new soul brother continued, "and with the stupid bleeding hearts who say it's wrong to call a slob a slob. What else would any civilized person call folks who litter their sidewalks and ours with whiskey bottles, greasy bones, and banana peels? Like your angry lady, however, I am way past the name-calling stage. Also past the stage of wanting to spray their side of One Hundredth Street with an Uzi. Now I think in terms of herding them all into a big slaughterhouse on the waterfront. You know—Dr. Demento's revenge. One by one they would be dragged before my throne to answer one critical question, within five seconds or else: 'Do you have any social graces whatsoever?'

"Being bound and gagged on arrival, very few of them could manage to beat the deadline."

We had reached our front stoop under a concrete overhang. The enemy camp, as seedy as the Bowery, was just across the street, drums and all.

Reno, glaring across no man's land, drew himself up and scowled. El Exigente in blackface. "So I let them have it. I say, 'Since you slobs are hopelessly insensitive . . . *adiós.*' My finger stabs a red button on the armrest of my throne, activating my bongo-disposal device. Presto! A trapdoor opens near the slobs' feet, and . . .

"Down and down they go
clown by clown they flow
in a spin, never to drum again
after my magic action
called shove"

DEAR ADAM,

He did it again—cut me off at the pass and blew up my best intentions with an undermine. Mr. Charlie, of course. Who else?

There I was, writing a series of letters that probably strained the credibility of my color. I was trying to portray the old scalawag in human dimensions for a change. Vah-voom! He reverted to stereotype. I refer to his latest charge at Columbia University.

After a brief but bloody sequence of racial rumbles on campus one night, two university deans investigated. They interrogated twenty-four witnesses and combatants. Only one participant was deemed guilty of a punishable indiscretion:

"A white student who was reported to have shouted racial slurs," the official report said. No explanation was given for the visible cuts and bruises displayed by blacks.

Despite the biracial makeup of the investigating team, I had a gut-level conviction that Mr. Charlie had somehow set the parameters. Thus resensitized to his talent for Machiavellian sleaze, I began to perceive subtler white-collar crimes. On television, for example, I noticed all these prison scenes in which 98 percent of the convicts were white guys with good teeth. Now, you know the colors of 80 percent of all inmates in New York, New Jersey, and Connecticut prisons, right?

Putting the real statistical picture in those reels would mean giving more acting jobs to blacks and Latinos. Or should I believe the wily scoundrel when Mr. C. presents his case as a victim of prejudiced pressure groups? "If I did show a prison with more minority cons than whites, I'd be lynched without a trial. You pinko liberals and black rednecks would accuse me of perpetuating the negative stereotypes of you all."

Reserving judgment on that one for the moment, what about this second incriminating syndrome? In today's U.S. Army, the Pentagon says, 28 percent of the enlisted personnel are black. So how does Mr. Charlie explain the nearly all-white tableaux on the screen in dramas about the military? Don't minority soldiers ever kiss their wives and kids good-bye or try to pick up a date?

While you are drawing your own conclusions, please give what you think is the proper weight to a third case in point:

In a roman à clef comedy on Channel 13, Ossie Davis and Ruby Dee did a number on Hollywood casting. As a talented but usually unemployed black actress in New York, Miss Dee's character was elated in the opening scene. She had just been promised the role of Thomas Jefferson's historically and anatomically correct black mistress. In the closing scene, she hears the awful truth over the telephone. Her part has been given to an Italian sexpot, Mariana Sophalina. "You see, darling, a

Hollywood *gantzeh macher* elucidated, "Gregory Bushel has been signed for the Jefferson part. And out here, well, they're terribly sensitive over the thought—the possible repercussions, you know—of having a white man kissing a black woman on the screen."

DEAR ADAM,

It never ceases to amaze me how effectively a child can instruct us. My all-time favorite story goes like this:

After a long hot day on the sidewalks of New York as a TV street reporter, Adam's father wearily settled down in his overstuffed easy chair in their living room. He held a Tanqueray martini on the rocks in one hand; the latest edition of *Ebony* magazine in the other. Dinner wouldn't be ready for at least an hour. He had barely begun reading, however, when he felt a tug at his elbow. "Let's play a game, Dad," said a seven-year-old dynamo in short pants. "Come on, let's play."

His dad sighed, searching for an indefinite reprieve. "Uh . . . let's put it this way, Tiger," he temporized, turning a page . . . hold everything! The centerfold of his magazine was a map of the United States. "I've got an idea for a new game we can play."

The little boy beamed, always eager for adventure.

"Here's a map of our country. See? This is New York, there's New Jersey and Pennsylvania; way out west, Nevada, Arizona, and California. Now I'm going to turn this map into a puzzle." He ripped out the centerfold and tore it into twenty-odd scraps.

Adam looked on, fascinated.

"First you put all the pieces on the floor," his father advised, handing them over. "Then spread them out. If you can get all the states in exactly their right places, I'll give you a dollar for your piggy bank."

Adam kneeled on the living-room rug, set to meet the challenge.

To hide a smug grin, the clever man took another sip of his martini. There, he thought, that should keep the little guy busy until dinnertime.

Wrong.

"Look, Dad, I did it," the little guy boasted scarcely three minutes later.

His father blinked, utterly astounded. The map was absolutely perfect. "Okay, Tiger. Well done. Here's your dollar. Now tell me something: How did you work it out so quickly?"

"It was easy," the boy said with a chuckle. "On the other side of the map, there's a picture of this large black family. When you get the black family right, our country's right."

DEAR MR. SKEPTIC:

Your reaction on the phone to my brief against wolfpacks, while not totally negative, was not the ringing endorsement that I had expected. Never mind. It just so happens that I now have the compelling necessities to bring you the rest of the way. Tonight while scanning my collection of old headlines that reek with either historical significance or buffoonery, I found one atop a story that covers both:

> **BLACK COP REJECTS OWN PROMOTION TO SERGEANT**
>
> A black police officer has turned down a promotion to sergeant, because, "I don't believe in racial quotas." Samuel Brown, a 14-year veteran, said his promotion had not been earned. He had failed to pass the Civil Service test.

Let's give a big high five to Officer Brown. His sense of honesty, pride, and dignity cost him seven thousand dollars a year. You can't make that much on welfare.

How could anybody call himself a man if he behaved less honorably than Officer Brown? This is America. Many, many doors are open, and you have a right to earn your way. Is there any other avenue to self-respect?

Hang on. The wolfpacks are coming back into focus. Mr. Brown had been among ninety-four blacks and eighty-nine Hispanics who were elevated to sergeant. A federal court had so ordered despite their embarrassing test scores. All had fallen below the generous cutoff point for minority candidates, 65.3. The cutoff for whites was 79.2. That means a bunch of white cops got shafted. I, for one, do not relish that brand of revenge.

What kind of guidance do you suppose those black and Hispanic dummies had received from their parents? In school, had they been students or wiseguys? Isn't it fair to say that only dumb wiseguys run with wolfpacks?

Above all, how could they deliberately humiliate themselves and their races by accepting rewards that they admit to being too stupid to deserve? Don't give me any of that cop-out lip about "white bias" in job tests. That's at least 90.6 percent baloney. Whites have no lock on books and other learning tools. All candidates must make an effort, however, to find and use those tools. No matter what prize is at stake in which arena, you simply husband your time and prepare your mind. I am confident that the white candidates who passed the test for sergeant had done nothing more devious than that.

So I ask once again: When are black and Hispanic laggards going to grasp the inescapable logic of their current demands for easier tests? In effect, they are running with the wolfpacks and telling Mr. Charlie that that bumbling old ex-Dodger Al Campanis had gotten it right after all: They "just don't have the necessities."

I wonder, Adam, how that celebrated baseball anthropologist would have evaluated your granddad. (You were only three years old when you last saw and conquered your favorite wrestling opponent.) I remind you that my father had to quit school and go to work at age twelve, driving a team of mules on a road-construction gang. His large family in rural Tennessee needed all the help they could get.

When I was a kid in the mid-thirties in Paris, Tennessee, Dad was earning seven dollars a week as an auto-body repairman. Being a skilled mechanic, he rebuilt a wrecked '32 Chevy that he had picked up for less than eight bars of a song. With one of the rare set of working wheels in our ghetto, he supplemented his income in three ways:

(a) as deliveryman for a whiskey distribution firm whose illegal distillery was a few miles out of town;

(b) by running a predawn taxi service for two schoolteachers whose rustic classrooms were beyond the limits of public transportation;

(c) by hunting, fishing, and selling his overkill to neighbors—twenty-five cents for a fat catfish or a rabbit; twenty cents for a squirrel, and fifteen cents for a quail.

That was serious money in those Depression years. You could buy a loaf of bread for ten cents. A hamburger cost a nickel.

As an only child in the midst of all that plenty, I honestly did not realize until years later, in my teens, that we had been among the poor.

In the late thirties, we moved north. Dad quickly found work in an auto-body shop at sixty-five bucks a week. I thought that we were on our way to becoming rich. In the mid-forties, he established his own repair shop. Ran it with moderate success until he retired at the age of sixty-six.

Knowing what my old man had achieved, how could I have faced him or myself if I failed to prove that I was worthy of being called his son?

DEAR JUDGE ADAM:

Our latest brief encounter was more like a head-on collision. So it was with your granddad and me when I was around your age. I deemed his point of view obsolete.

I can see how you might have misinterpreted or otherwise rejected some recent sayings by Chairman Dad. You might have heard what you regarded as proof of Mr. Charlie's skills as a ventriloquist. Okay. I admit to having said stuff that you only expect to hear from the likes of him. However, there is mutiny in my apparent meekness. Trust me.

The point of my viewpoint is, we could better deal with him if we gained a fuller catalog of his vulnerabilities. We have been too busy cataloging his sign language instead.

First, we should acknowledge that, right or wrong, Mr. C. feels what he feels. To ignore that is to miss opportunities for meaningful communication, and someday perhaps a mutual-assistance pact. Think back to all the honorable settlements between old adversaries. With the arguable exceptions of Attila the Hun and Hitler, one's enemies can also claim roots in the human family. Therefore they are reachable. I am not talking about card-carrying white liberals. I am saying that there a lot of fair-minded uncommitted whites out there. To enlist them, all we have to do is quit pretending that they are solely to blame for all the ugly pieces in the motley mosaic of America.

If Your Honor pleases, may the defense introduce a couple of old headlines? So help me, these two beauties appeared on page seven of the *New York Post*:

VIGILANTE OR VICTIM?

GOETZ TRIAL BEGINS

FIVE MUGGERS PICK

WRONG TIME, PLACE

You already know about Bernie Goetz. The other story was more routine, less publicized. A wolfpack from the Bedford-Stuyvesant ghetto in Brooklyn, rampaging in Manhattan, attacked a sixty-eight-year-old grandfather near the New York Hilton Hotel. The overwhelming odds against the victim quickly changed, however. About two thousand Roman Catholic cops just happened to be leaving the Hilton after a Holy Name Society breakfast. Guess how many surprised black sprinters finished in jail?

"Ah, but what about the likes of Ivan Boesky and Dennis Levine?" you ask, recalling headlines about dozens of multimillionaire robber barons on Wall Street. Yes, and there are rogues and extortionists in the industrial-military complex, visibly assisted by my-hand-is-out politicians. I also share your indignation over the Supreme Court's ruling that we have to live with the death penalty even though black killers of whites are eleven times more likely to be legally snuffed than white killers of blacks.

Indignation is no substitute, however, for practical consequences. That is what I am about here. We need stronger stuff to create better breaks for the Roosevelt Johnsons and José Rodriguezes of our time. As President Kennedy once observed, "Life is unfair." Some individuals start out with bigger handicaps and/or assets than others. You only kid yourself if you hold your breath and pout. No caped crusader is going to spring out of nowhere to intervene. So the sensible thing to do is to take action that is based on an honest adult appraisal of the problem. To wit: Mr. Charlie.

Take a peek inside his psyche. See? He harbors no fear of the crooks who pull big rip-offs with telephones, computers, and snake oil. (The late Willie Sutton and the missing skyjacker D. B. Cooper are folk heroes, right?) It is those crude bozos out there with knives, Saturday night specials and loosely laced sneakers who upset Mr. Charlie. They scare me, too.

What I am driving at here is, you have a better chance of working something out with your enemy if you start by admitting that you are somewhat as ludicrous as he. In my experience, only when the two sides could laugh at each other and at themselves did a real chance develop for respect.

DEAR ADAM,

In the lexicon of black copycats, the prospect of facing Mr. Charlie without verbally blunt instruments is risky business; like inviting Jaws to lunch. However, in a dream I had the other night—interviewing Mr. C. on prime-time network television—I saw an alternative black future. It was brighter than anything we have seen up to now. It was clear that no new technology would be required to develop a very effective weapon for our battle against the unnatural order of what is. I am talking again about listening with our third ear.

In my dream interview, Mr. Charlie—annoyed and impatient—sketched his prime concerns. Staggering stuff. Considering their magnitude from his perspective, you can begin to appreciate his indolence to our prime concerns.

The scene: A brightly lit TV studio in Rockefeller Center. Two wheel-based TK-44 cameras, anachronisms from the sixties, are being muscled across the waxed vinyl floor by two husky technicians wearing jump suits. Presently, the cumbersome old cameras, with snouts like the barrels of howitzers, are ready to shoot, juxtaposed for a video crossfire.

Mr. Charlie and I amble onto the set. Somberly we take our places on backless stools, old gladiators glaring at each other. No pretenses. A pretty female stage manager fastens minimikes to our neckties. As she backs off into the shadows, an off-camera announcer, his voice as deep as thunder, rumbles pompously: "What you are about to see on Channel Four and One-fifth, ladies and gentlemen, is not a real program. It's just TV."

My cue. "First of all, Mr. Charlie, what in the world could possibly be preventing you from seeing that nothing is more urgent than . . ."

"Don't ask," he interrupts in the manner of a spoiled pooh-bah. "I've got no time for trivial pursuit. You are looking at a victim of outrageous circumstances that transcend my faults. I am trapped in a muddy scenario in which black is just another ambiguous shade of gray.

"Over here and over there, morons with easy access to nuclear triggers are trying like hell to get a war on.

"My rich Uncle Sam, the last time I checked, had two-point-four trillion dollars less than no money at all.

"The worst drugs are destroying the nicest neighborhoods.

"God seems to be AWOL.

"Among my closest friends and relatives, respectable charlatans are being busted almost everywhere; even the basement of the White House is not safe anymore.

"That is not the worst of it by a foul shot. Every time one of us appears on television in unflattering dishabille—like handcuffs—our image is unjustly tarnished by odious comparisons with black and Latino creeps.

"Sex is screwed up, too. Less fun for everybody harboring serious doubts about diseases.

"To maintain my power—my lawyers say—I must train my forked tongue to speak Japanese, Chinese, and OPEC.

"I can't sock a punk or a drunk anymore without being sued for my share of the GNP.

"Wherever I try to dump my garbage, watchdogs start foaming at the mouth and growling, 'Stick it where the sun don't shine.'

"All of us in the white majority have yet to learn how to live happily ever after with toxic waste.

"Licensed extortionists are charging scandalous prices for the privilege of breathing, eating, and drinking all the wrong stuff.

"I haven't found a legal parking space since 1959.

"Television ads are sponsoring unrealistic expectations among the undeserving masses.

"Federal judges insist on curbing my rights to exploit the powerless.

"In other words, day by day another parasitic privilege that supports my lubricious life-style goes Humpty-Dumpty."

Mr. Charlie paused and blew his nose dramatically. "I am talking real problems here; sitting on the edge of belly-up. Now that you know what I'm up against, all I can say to minorities who perceive themselves as God's children at the center of the universe is this: May the farce be with you."

Fade to black.

DEAR WOUNDED SURVIVOR FROM A BROKEN HOME:

In another of my recurring daydreams of life in the promised land, I see marching regiments of black refugees from shattered families like ours. They are striving to recover, picking themselves up and getting back in the race to catch the 7:19 from Larchmont to success.

Furthermore, I see an eloquent extension of my persona persuading young dudes like you to pounce on any chance to go to college.

I have yet to confirm my theory that maybe your no-college-now stance was some sort of protest—or an expression of pain. Like the body blows you must have felt during the disintegration of our family. I shared that pain. Which perhaps explains the distraction that prevented me from communicating to you some of the unadvertised rewards of higher learning, regardless of whatever other goals one may pursue. When you were younger I focused too narrowly on the link between education and employment and the need to accumulate money as a shield against the worst improprieties of racism. I should have been selling the poetry, beauty, and magic that education brings to one's life and the way it stirs the soul. And the learning process continues, with escalating diversity, at higher speeds. In my experience, the relationships between things, events, ideas, and circumstances became less puzzling, more instructive. I began to recognize patterns, anomalies, mistakes, and triumphs of civilized folks over the centuries. I began to anticipate errors and disasters, then profit from my perceptions. More important, I began to experience the heady elation that comes with the effort to create ideas and works of art.

94   To make amends for my oversight, I yearn to find some supernatural technique to implant a little magic in the brains of disadvantaged children. I am talking about the kind of magic that would lift their aspirations well beyond their current popular desire to become rich and famous as members of yet another jiving bastard-rhyming rap group. At the same time, I want to see black parents working up raps of their own to steer their kids onto the right tracks. "Would you like to discuss some ways and means that might help you to stop flushing your life down the toilet?" Or, "As long as you are under this roof, you will obey the house rules."

Somehow I must sell the excitement of learning. I am thinking now about my freshman course in Zoology 1 at Wisconsin more than thirty-five years ago. It astonished me to see certain animals, untrained by man, using tools.

A predatory fish, hovering just below the surface of a river, spits water against the underside of leaves that overhang the water, the idea being to dislodge insects squatting topside. Once the little buggers hit the surface—gulp!

An African chimp pokes a skinny stick into an underground colony of living hors d'oeuvres; when he retracts the stick, it is crawling with delicious captives. Gulp!

A huge bird lays an egg so tough she has to pick up a marble-sized rock with her beak and fling it at the egg, again and again, to break the shell and hatch her little darling.

A clever otter carries a flat rock when he dives for oysters; upon returning to the surface with a closed oyster shell in his mouth, he floats on his back, balances the rock on his tummy, and slams the shellfish against it with both paws. Gulp!

Think for a moment, speculate. What different bright ideas might have eventually come to me and my classmates after becoming aware of such phenomena? Isn't it amazing what college professors—the Svengalis of civilization—can do with the magic of ideas? They fill young brains with the stuff that creates more room for thinking.

Maybe I should have hired a task force of Madison Avenue consultants to arouse lust in your heart for an alma mater. Or maybe I should have updated a family legend that defined the peer pressure that nudges adolescents into the mainstream. Long, long ago, your great-granddaddy told me when I was a boy, our tribal ancestors in Africa invented sort of a practical bar mitzvah for young blacks. To achieve manhood, around sixteen years of age each aspiring hunter-warrior faced a dangerous test. Alone, he had to trek into the bush, armed with only a spear, and kill a lion. Or die. Since the tribe could neither prosper nor survive without a steady supply of tough buck privates trained to hunt animals and fight men, every institution within the tribe herded the unsuspecting prospects into the prep school. That was the magic in their lives—the basis of their hopes for a long

and happy tomorrow. To be on that track meant status. Not to be meant disgrace. Scarcely anyone dared to risk a lifetime of diminished respect from their friends and neighbors. Such a fate, the boys were taught from infancy, would truly be worse than death. So they willingly enrolled—dedicating themselves to acquiring discipline, skill, knowledge, courage, and stamina to earn their place in the tribe. And they stayed the course. Dropping out was unthinkable. Eventually, they were prepared to face whatever challenge might threaten their people.

If I'm lucky, I will find a way to translate that legend into the language of the nineties. Gradually, black families would develop the necessary auxiliary concepts and institutions to support the new legend: In order to become a respected and useful member of our tribe, young blacks must strive for and scheme for even the skinniest chance to reach college, because everybody knows that's where it's at.

DEAR MR. NO JOE COLLEGE:

Your first cousin Barbara called tonight from Harvard with happy news. On the verge of being crowned with an Ivy League mortar board, she has landed a job: Trainee reporter for Long Island *Newsday*. A damn prestigious rag.

I am therefore inviting you to a small dinner party that Lady Jan and I are planning for next Saturday night to make a big fuss over Barbara.

No, I am not rubbing it in that you have yet to enroll in college. Look at all the money I am saving. Lady Jan and I will be vacationing in Hawaii next month, thanks to you. I simply want to share family pride in my favorite niece. She is sharp enough now to work as a TV reporter at some D-market station in the boondocks. No kidding. I know because two summers ago she accompanied me and other NBC veterans on a number of assignments. Judging from her performance in make-believe stand-uppers that were taped by my colleagues, judging too from the savvy questions that she asked us in the field, Barbara is one of those articulate, beautiful young people who seem to have been born for the tube.

However, having accepted the advice of her doting uncle, she is first going to master the nuts and bolts of news biz in print; just like me. Which means that when she does switch to TV after a few hundred bylines straight ahead, she will be more than just another pretty face with sex appeal. She will be a solid hard-nosed journalist. I would call that upholding a family tradition.

The next time I accept a speaking engagement in one of our dead-end neighborhoods, I am going to talk about a role model named Barbara: The inspiring saga of a female Horatio Alger in living color. Though raised in a dangerous drug-infested gulch in Brooklyn, this determined young lady has made some sensible choices. Among others, heeding the wisdom of her caring, hardworking parents. Which helped her to beat the odds. It is a rare person of any color who can climb onto the elevated tracks that lead to success without a head start like that.

The moral is, give me ten thousand Barbaras a year for the next quarter-century, and I guarantee it: We shall overcome.

TO MY SON THE IMPRESARIO:

I caught your show on Channel D tonight. At first I couldn't believe it was happening: An original half-hour comedy with seven characters created, produced, and directed for TV by my Adam. My Big Guy. A little rough around the edges in almost every scene, sure. It was a commendable rookie effort, however. So don't feel that you have to apologize.

Of course being on a public-access channel is not the same as being on a commercial station. The point is, you stepped out there and made an effort. You are certainly going to sharpen your writing skills and tighten the reins on the actors you direct. Next time.

My deepest satisfaction came from knowing what diverse and difficult disciplines you had to learn to get that far. Clearly, you are on your way in the right direction. The less-traveled road that you have taken—to be the maven in control—is the right one. I wish that more young blacks would follow. The world at large is much more prone to see things your way if you are in the catbird seat.

You can therefore understand my anger over the news story I covered today. It was the inaugural semester of a Black Studies major at Columbia University. That kind of major, I submit, does not lead to the executive suite or a seat on the board of directors. I think it is high time to reevaluate our academic priorities. What do you suppose might happen to the black unemployment rate if the next generation of job applicants could offer their services to companies being managed by distant cousins? If you were in a position to hire, would you go with an expert on black history or with a broadly educated dude who could program a computer, speak a foreign language, and direct a huge research project?

Am I saying that black studies ought to be ignored? Of course not. To be informed about and proud of one's heritage is important. To let it distract you from acquiring more utilitarian skills, however, is pathetic.

We would be wise, I think, to follow a Jewish example in this instance. Our news program aired a story last week about a Holocaust Studies program in the Bronx High School of Science. A one-semester course. The teenagers who were interviewed seemed to be grasping the awful facts and what they meant. Their curriculum includes dramatic workshops in which the students take turns playing Nazis and *Juden,* using scripts from the pages of infamy.

A Holocaust major for college students, in their judgment and mine, would be tantamount to overkill.

DEAR ADAM,

He did it to me again—cut me off at the knees and stabbed me in the back. No, not Mr. Charlie. I give you, with deep regret, Mr. Slender Black or Hispanic Male in His Early Twenties.

There I was, writing a series of conciliatory letters, encouraging détente between races, when— *whammo!* Our roving anti-goodwill ambassador inserted himself into an unsavory plethora of police interviews on Channel 4.

"The suspect is a slender black or Hispanic male who . . .

"(a) stabbed a nun to death during a burglary,

"(b) robbed and raped several white females in well-to-do neighborhoods;

"(c) wounded six New York cops in a shootout before vanishing in a housing project whose residents saw him as a hero;

"(d) stomped a seventy-four-year-old Hispanic man to death;

"(e) set fire to an apartment to cover up the double murder of his common-law wife and their infant daughter;

"(f) strangled a female invalid who had hired him to take care of her shopping and push her wheelchair to the nearest clinic;

"(g) et cetera."

Take a wild guess: How many of our white allies, reacting with their instincts to those horrifics, felt an impulse to renew their membership in the Klan?

Sure, everybody knows that black violence maims and destroys more blacks than anybody else. Hispanic violence ditto. In even the most liberal pragmatic heart, however, those facts are not reassuring. "Ye Gods," the yuppies ask one another, "if they'll do all that to one another, what in the blue-eyed world might they do to real human beings like us?"

Am I asking my black and Latino soulmates to retreat from injustice in abject cowardice? Of course not. I am begging them to fight back smart, not stupid.

To achieve our ultimate goals, will we advance faster or slower if we consistently point a finger at Mr. Charlie as the root of all our troubles, never at ourselves? It is my guess that true progress now depends on abandoning our current posture of total innocence. I say we have more to gain than Mr. Charlie does by blinking first. What is wrong with backing down a little if the end result is a great leap closer to the promised land? With assistance.

In the advanced stage of my schizophrenia, I have a recurring nightmare. The scene is the next Olympic Games. Only two athletes will compete; the nations of the world have formally agreed on the political prize at stake. If the minority contestant wins as many gold medals as the champion of white supremacy, racism will cheerfully be banished everywhere.

You guessed it. Our deus ex machina, boldly certified by his will alone, is Mr. Slender Black or Hispanic Male in His Early Twenties. On the eve of the crucial competition, he either shoves two hundred bucks' worth of coke up his nose, goes on a rampage with a wolfpack, or forges his signature on somebody else's welfare check. *¡Caramba!*

DEAR ADAM,

Your defection from the public-school system at age fourteen, after six weeks of trial and terror, makes more sense now because of current developments on that violent crack-infested front. Wisely, you gave up on the High School of Music and Art to avoid sudden death or permanent injury. Which you surely could have suffered in those daily food fights in the cafeteria that invariably escalated to "plastic-tray wars" at point-blank range. So . . . back you went into the cocoon of the expensive private-school sector.

Today, seven years later, the city's first black schools chancellor, Richard Green, officially authorized the use of airport-style metal detectors in five high schools. "Something has to be done," he acknowledged with chagrin, to curb the influx of .357-magnum revolvers, cheap Saturday night specials, kung fu throwing stars, gravity knives, brass knuckles, and so-called pin guns that fire .22-caliber bullets. Teachers and security officers had confiscated 1,495 such weapons in New York's public junior and senior high schools during the 1986–87 academic year. The number of shooting incidents among teenagers, in school and on the street, keeps rising like a skyrocket. Said the beleaguered principal of West Side High: "They are selling guns like candy bars."

It came as no surprise, then, when the Board of Education president Bobby Wagner, Jr., endorsed the chancellor's strategy in these words: "Schools should be weapon-free zones." Man, what a breakthrough in academic philosophy!

Yesterday, on a subway train in Brooklyn, seven black high school students and dropouts were involved in a shooting. A gang of six, using a headlock on their victim, mauled and robbed seventeen-year-old DeCosta Wright on his way home from school. After being stripped of his three-finger gold ring, wallet, and twenty dollars, Wright got tough and did something wrong: Pulling a .25 automatic, he shot the one who was trying to rip off his sneakers. The rest fled.

DeCosta, a serious student at Pacific High with no police record, was hauled off to jail: Assault, reckless endangerment, and illegal possession of a gun.

His stepfather defended the boy with three short sentences that broke my heart: "He's been beat up before. He's been attacked twice . . . recently. And he probably felt a need to protect himself."

The robbery victim's classmates at Pacific High told the media that approximately half of the four hundred students there carried guns. Some did it for self-defense; others, to cope with competitors in the crack trade. The following quotation from one slender minority male student made me weep for a whole generation of youngsters in New York: "Let's say I'm dealing drugs, and you're coming to my high school to deal drugs. I ain't gonna go for that. I got my gun, and you're crossing over into my turf. Or if you're dealing more crack than I am"—pause, laconic shrug—"you gotta go."

How can we build a better tomorrow if we prey upon our brothers every day?

TO ADAM THE SORE LOSER:

Pending hard evidence to the contrary, I shall assume that your failure to keep our tennis date last weekend was unavoidable. Nothing to do with the 6–0, 6–1 score of our last match, right? No connection either to your grudging admission that "maybe" your old man has come up with a valid point in Mr. Charlie's favor.

I hereby submit further corroboration of my hypothesis that there is a regiment of upright whites out there—rarely publicized chaps who have marched that extra mile to help us gain a foot.

The story I covered early this evening for *News 4 New York* at eleven was a fund-raising dinner at the Hilton. The sponsor was the Interracial Council for Business Opportunity. Never heard of them, you say? I don't doubt it. Good news gets short shrift in TV news (which should not be confused with journalism). Well, this council is a beautiful rainbow, Jesse Jackson style. More than eight hundred corporate executives and business leaders belong. Committed, they say, to "nonwhite enterprise development." They don't mean kitchens and bodegas. And lip service is not their long suit. For twenty-four years, they have been helping nonwhites to acquire and expand their own pieces of the action. Would you believe fifty thousand clients so far?

Council members donate valuable time, talent, and financial backup. They are proud of the many success stories behind their efforts. Lee Dunham, for example, owns four McDonald's franchises in New York. Then there is the New Jersey Paste & Glue Company. The Harlem-based Consolidated Beverage Corporation, also owned and operated by blacks, distributes beer and colas. Its president, Albert Thompson, was honored as Minority Businessman of the Year.

My favorite quote at the dinner came from the council's CEO Malcolm Corrin: "Each new business success mentored by the council means that we have more role models for the young to look up to and emulate."

On the theory that you are somewhat impressed by the council's good works, my son, I ask you to reconsider one of my heretical dogmas in a new context. Think of yourself as a slender black male in his early twenties who is handcuffed to an eight-hundred-pound gorilla named Mr. Charlie. Being comfortable where he is, why should this ugly lump of stubbornness have a smidgen of interest in going your way? Should you press your point by calling him a dumb ape and kicking him in the shins?

Or would you have better luck if you invited your eight-hundred-pound neighbor to share a stalk of ripe bananas? What if you asked him to join you and Cleveland Amory in a nonviolent counterassault on gorilla-bashers?

110

CONGRATU-LATE ME, ADAM:

I have invented a word. It capsulizes my contempt for nonsense of any color: *satob*. Meaning sick and tired of bullshit, it can be conjugated like a Latin verb: satobo, satobas, satobat, satobatus, sabotatis, satobant.

The concept congealed today as I covered the pretrial news conference held by a clever white lawyer named Jack Litman. He is defending a con- fessed white killer named Robert Chambers. First, Litman asked us hard-boiled cynics to swallow a rather tasteless alibi: His yuppie client had uninten- tionally strangled a young female half his size when she refused to stop squeezing his testicles during sadomasochistic foreplay.

Most of us grimaced, but none of us vomited. Litman took that as a mandate to keep going. With the demeanor of a born-again Christian, he sug- gested that the late Jennifer Levin had been a tramp. Her diary would prove as much if the court would only grant his motion to turn it over to him. It therefore followed, he implied, that she probably had gotten what she deserved.

"Jack Litman," a white radio commentator observed, "is a white version of C. Vernon Mason and Alton Maddox."

Mind you, there are no blacks, except Judge Howard Bell, in this murder case. What I'm getting at is my deep-seated prejudice against lawyers. Those who call themselves prosecutors and judges are no exceptions. After covering hundreds of criminal trials for television, I feel loathing and contempt for the immoral majority of them. My impression is that the opposing legal eagles have only a pro forma interest in truth or justice. What they seek more than anything else is victory. The spoils include a larger share of the desperate-client market and higher fees; eventually, sinecures on the bench.

Judges, of course, are willing co-conspirators in the nasty games that lawyers play with people's lives. They show no qualms about the legal gimmicks that suppress critical evidence. Yes, I know, the suppressed stuff can be brought up in cross-examination or redirect. But if I were a judge, I would not sit still while a witness was being gagged by legal tricks—prevented from telling the whole truth. As in, "The witness will answer yes or no."

Oh, sure. Our devil's-advocate system makes them do it. Hah. Who do you suppose invented that system centuries ago and has steadfastly refused to pass laws to reform it? Legislatures dominated by lawyers.

Several years earlier I had seen Jack Litman equally singleminded in the role of assistant district attorney. In the very same courtroom where he is now defending a confessed murderer, he once nailed a rogue cop, Officer William Phillips, for murder. Instead of feeling even a little bit guilty over his current affronts to reason, my style, Litman displays the aplomb of a hit man. As if to say, "Nothing personal, old bean. Just business. If I don't get the blighter off, you know, someone else will."

I have ground away a quarter-inch of molars over that traditional stance. It is convoluted sophistries of that ilk, I think, that have corrupted our once-promising civilization. Every "officer of the court," as they claim to be, has a higher responsibility, I believe. They ought to care whether what they do in a trial will result in giving truly dangerous characters a few more shots at the rest of us. I mean, are your rights to be left alone—unharmed and unrobbed—any less precious than the rights of convicted terrorists on parole?

Isn't there something asinine and impractical about unleashing two-legged jackals simply because they confessed before the cops read aloud the judicial loopholes created by the Miranda decision?

Ergo, I feel satobic. Like being dunked against my will in a mull-again stew of anger and disgust.

Satobia also reared its ugly head twice one day as I covered related stories in Harlem and the Crown Heights section of Brooklyn. First, a public hearing in the State Office Building on 125th Street. The governor's Task Force on Bias-Related

Violence was listening to a litany of horrors: A proliferation of attacks on blacks, Hispanics, Jews, Asians, gays, et al.

Ah, here we go again, I grumbled. The latest statistics showed a 300 percent increase in racially motivated attacks in the New York area this year. Mr. Charlie was reacting with typical ado worth nothing: Public hearing No. 2,986 on a problem that refused to stay buried under tons of bureaucratic reports on previous public hearings.

Come on, admit it. Makes you feel a bit satobic too.

Anyway, I barely restrained myself from applauding as two black ministers, testifying at least three hours apart, said, in effect: Who are you guys trying to kid?

Said the Reverend Calvin Butts, "History tells me that the first of these commission hearings on racism was held here in Harlem in the 1920s."

Reverend Wendell Foster, a city councilman, added later, "This commission could save a lot of time by cancelling these hearings. I suggest instead that you simply read the Kerner Report of the sixties. It's all in there. Racism remains as alive and well as it was back then. . . ."

What we need now, both ministers argued in weary, pessimistic voices, is leadership from the mayor, the governor, and the president. They should be for job-training programs, affirmative action, and vigorous enforcement of existing protections under the law.

The mayor, the governor, and the president were and still are otherwise engaged.

Moving on to the Crown Heights story . . .

My satobilic antennae twitched as I interviewed a white detective in the antibias unit. Hasidic youth, he said, had firebombed a black family's home; they felt that it was too close to their religious sect's headquarters on Eastern Parkway.

As you have probably deduced by now, my son, satobia is what I was trying to convey in previous letters about allegedly biased qualifying tests. Which means, in many black and Latino manifestos, any test in which white competitors compile embarrassingly superior numbers.

What about the embarrassingly superior numbers compiled year after year by the Michael Jordans, Dr. J's, and Kareem Abdul Jabbars in the NBA? Suppose all the white players who fail to match them cried "Foul." Would you favor letting them shoot at a separate hoop that was larger and closer to the floor?

Should white running backs in the NFL be given a twelfth man to block on every carry?

How about a twenty-yard head start for white base stealers in the majors?

And why not allow great white hopes to bring pick handles into the ring?

DEAR ADAM,

On the theory that selected young black and Hispanic dropouts can be channeled into the mainstream if granted a halfway decent opportunity, an altruistic white businessman of my acquaintance recently hired half a dozen of that disreputable lot.

Alas. They have gradually persuaded me that his theory is somewhat flawed.

The neophytes, along with young whites, alternate as drivers and dispatchers for Jerry's Rainbow Limousine Service. His storefront office is on the block across the street from the apartment house where Lady Jan and I reside in separate flats. We had long ago developed the habit of going on the town via Rainbow: A fleet of well-maintained upscale vehicles and competent personnel. After the colorization of the staff, we made five pickup appointments in a span of three weeks. In the luck of the draw, familiar white faces showed up behind the steering wheels for our first two excursions—to a cocktail party and a Broadway play. On the next two trips, we rode with two strangers who apparently were operating on C.P. (Colored People's Time). How in the hell did they manage to drive their cars from the middle of the block across the street to my front door at least ten minutes tardy? Mentally, I put the whole outfit on probation.

Which brings us to last night. My lady and I, looking for a Rainbow once again, waited seven minutes under our canopy for nought. Which ruined the timing for her surprise birthday party. Close friends who had kept the secret were waiting in ambush in a posh midtown restaurant.

Through the office window across the street, I could see three dudes who struck me as their own worst enemies: The dispatcher who had logged my appointment and my previous two tardy chauffeurs. Leaving Lady Jan under the canopy, I stalked over there gritting my teeth. Steam was gushing from every orifice.

"Good evening, gentlemen," I growled in my unmistakably unfriendly mode. Sarcasm would have been wasted on those lallygaggers. I let 'em have both barrels between the eyes. "I just came over to tell you guys how you just lost one of Jerry's regular customers. By-not-taking-care-of-business." My deliberately measured cadence between clenched molars seemed to nudge them off-balance. They blinked without replying, their faces blank. "I came in here at six-fifteen this morning on my way to work. I ordered a car for seven-fifty this evening. At my front door across the street. And-you-guys-found-some-STUPID-WAY-TO-BLOW-IT."

The dispatcher, having glanced down at the ledger on the counter in front of him, stirred lethargically. "Oh, yeah," he conceded without the slightest hint of apology. "You did make a contract and we do have a car for you."

I snorted and harrumphed my contempt. "I'm sure you do. But you didn't have it where it was supposed to be at seven-fifty P.M."

I wheeled out of there and didn't look back. It wasn't necessary to inform them that my disaffection was irreversible. Less than a minute later, I flagged down a professional driver in a yellow cab and saved about ten dollars.

If you embrace the notion that white is not always right, you have to agree that black is not always beautiful, and respond accordingly.

118

DEAR ADAM,

What would you say if I confessed that lately, deeper than ever in my fifties, I have felt a resonance in my schizoid soul with Mr. Charlie? His, too, is a split personality. I believe that I am finally able to assimilate a more realistic picture of the enemy without, after learning some years ago to shake hands with the enemy within.

Perhaps I can exploit that resonance. A better reading of Mr. Charlie's intentions could result. Consider, for example, the super Nielsen ratings that white America is currently bestowing upon the *Cosby* sitcom and the Oprah Winfrey talk show. Week after month after year, they are blowing the competition away. White competition, I hasten to add. Why should black performers attract more attention from predominantly white audiences than white performers in similar vehicles?

It occurs to me that Mr. Charlie is trying to send us a message. Take note, he is saying, that neither Cosby nor Winfrey are one-dimensional blacks. They conduct themselves in ways that demonstrate their awareness of a sprawling universe beyond racism—a realm of wonder and dazzling possibilities. Their daily concerns on the tube are in synch with the daily concerns of decent Americans of any color. Perhaps paramount in significance, though, are the sensible compromises they have graciously made, which clearly enable them to live more comfortably in two cultures.

Think of their conduct, grammar, posture, grooming, and sense of values. Is it fair to say that, to some degree, Mr. Charlie's culture is reflected? Isn't it also obvious, however, that Oprah and Cosby's TV family also reflect their black heritage in all of those relevant categories?

Consider, too, that Cosby and his TV wife portray take-charge parents. By the second commercial break it becomes quite clear that Mom and Dad Huxtable are not going to tolerate childish nonsense as a way of life. They dictate family policy. Disruptive behavior in or outside the home is verboten.

So the cryptogram from Mr. Charlie translates into: "Black folks of that caliber are always welcome in my society—graduated, assimilated, and not on welfare."

What profit can we gain from this intelligence report? I say, face it, first of all. Don't waste indignation on the unfairness of his power to dictate standards. Instead, work up a game plan based on the knowledge that Mr. Charlie is much more prone to consider better ideas like yours if you first make an effort to excel within existing racist guidelines.

Personally, en route to one success after another with less and less opposition, I adopted this rule: Never demand a job, a meal ticket, or respect. Instead, establish expertise and honesty, with a little moxie and a lot of common sense. That is the way to go and keep on going to reach your goals. Believe me, when you get whatever you have demanded, no matter how big, it is always considerably less than what you get when you have earned it.

P.S. Add symptoms of schizophrenia: Reading the above paragraphs, I am simultaneously encouraged and disturbed. I realize how heretical some of my ideas may sound to preconditioned black ears. Which reminds me of the day I covered the assassination of Malcolm X, my number-one hero, in February 1965.

As you undoubtedly recall from my periodic tributes to the man, Malcolm had wisely recanted the white-man-is-the-devil mythology of the Black Muslim leader Elijah Muhammed. After a fact-finding mission to the Middle East, he came home inspired—preaching a fresh view of Islam. Forget that total-separation-of-the-races nonsense, he said. His new vision of Islam permitted and encouraged cooperation between blacks and whites.

Was it his heresy that beckoned orthodox Black Muslims to the Audubon Ballroom, with automatic weapons, that cold Sunday afternoon?

DEAR WUNDERKIND,

I said it on the phone when you gave me the good news last night. I want to say it again with ruffles and flourishes.

Your first paying gig in show biz, third banana in a Burger King commercial. Hot dog! Cousin Barbara is also impressed.

Aside from getting your act together, you also have shown grace under the pressure of being a winner. You frankly admitted that your luck as a part-time actor had changed dramatically when you gave up punk haircuts. I refrained from mentioning that on the phone. Didn't want to give the impression that I was saying, "See, I told you so."

I am writing about it now because that factor in your success has broad implications on a couple of fronts. Going against the mainstream is necessary in some situations, but a wise man knows that sometimes you can go faster and farther by going along with the tide. Second, if I am cajoling our hotheaded kinfolks to use their heads to get ahead of Mr. Charlie, shouldn't I also elaborate on the copyrighted techniques of black finesse?

Give me a minute. Maybe I'll think of something.

Meanwhile, please consider the implications of

one trenchant episode in your old man's odyssey in news biz: Dad versus an empty suit. Call him Baron Von Schmuck. Within a month after taking over as news boss at Channel 4, the baron decided to "shore up a weakness in our operation." His senior street reporter was thus condemned to permanent weekend depression. "For the foreseeable future," the little tyrant said with equanimity. "I need a real pro on the Saturday and Sunday newscasts."

Yep. He meant me.

"But Baron," I protested in his office, "we have a rotation of veterans on the weekends, set up by our previous news director. It was his idea of an 'egalitarian shop.' All of us in the pool—nine or ten, I think—are willing to live with that. But permanent weekend duty—for me, the guy with more seniority than anybody else in this shop, twenty-four years? I can't believe you're telling me that that's my reward."

Baron Von Schmuck didn't blink. "Oh, come off it," he commanded, an indulgent but impatient Dutch uncle. "Being assigned to work the weekends is not a punishment. You're overreacting."

Seeing no chance to get on his good side, I deliberately addressed him in a manner that showed disrespect. "That's beautiful, really beautiful. First you piss in my face, now you're telling me it's raining."

The Baron was steamed.

I worked six consecutive weekends, fuming.

He then reassigned me to my old Monday-Friday routine. Not because he had reconsidered the facts. Oh, no. He backed down because a couple of executives higher up had backed me up.

"You went over my head," Von Schmuck squealed like a wounded pig. "How could you do that to me?"

"Hey, man, I went to you first. You didn't get it."

So what is the point of that story? you ask. Just this: During my six weeks of corporate infighting with Von Schmuck, I never so much as hinted that his motives smacked of racism. I fought back strictly on the basis of the objective facts in the case, not on conjecture as to how he might have felt about interracial toilets. The well-bred upperclassmen who restored my salutary life-style—back to the tennis court on weekends—had interpreted the same facts my way. That is, Von Schmuck must have traded in his brain for a hat rack.

Since my problem had been the ninth or tenth load of the Baron's dung to be dumped upstairs that month, his superiors weighed alternatives for a few more days. Then they quietly told the man where he could go. On the day he announced his resignation in our hushed newsroom, a colleague asked me, "Did the Baron jump or was he pushed?"

"I don't know. But when he went through the door, there was a big footprint on the seat of his pants."

During the ensuing days of celebration in the newsroom, as in "Ding dong the witch is dead," I heard true tales of woe from many other Von

Schmuckophobiacs. Before and after being forced to get off my back, he had tried to saddle other veteran reporters with the permanent weekend gig. His hit list included one white male, one white female, one black female, and one Oriental female. They too had argued that the Baron either retain the rotation plan or go back to the news-biz tradition of stuffing the weekends with new turkeys.

I had come to realize that by that time that the Baron was a certifiable psychotic, incredibly autocratic and insensitive to every ethic except Machiavelli's. I felt pleased with myself for having resisted the old temptation to indict Von Schmuck for the wrong crime.

The bottom line, my son, is this educated guess by a trained professional observer: Among the villains we should worry about in this world, I suspect, there are many more Von Schmucks than Grand Dragons of the Ku Klux Klan.

Even if you disagree with my conclusion, surely you can see that it would not hurt our cause to attack Mr. Charlie once in a while on his blind side—for being stupid, incompetent, or off the wall.

DEAR ADAM,

My perception, and Gus Heningburg's, about parental fear of unruly children, has been corroborated once again, this time in the most horrifying manner conceivable. The story I covered this morning concerned Alonzo Williams, a seventeen-year-old high school dropout. He was charged with pumping five bullets into his mother, Rosie Williams, as she mopped the kitchen floor.

As District Attorney Ken Gribetz told the media, "The defendant had complained to people that his mother was picking on him, nagging him all the time."

In other words, she had been trying to straighten him out. So Alonzo had bought a .22-caliber rifle for one hundred fifty dollars last week, the DA added, telling his mother that he needed it for protection. Early Tuesday, after thirty-eight-year-old Rosie Williams returned from her night-shift job at the Elmwood Nursing Home, she decided to mop the kitchen. Her son came down the stairs with the rifle. "He opened fire while her back was turned."

Gribetz said Alonzo then went upstairs and hid the weapon before going to his part-time job as a messenger. "Shortly before noon, he came home and turned on the gas jets in the kitchen—a bungled attempt to burn down the house."

His two sisters discovered their mother's body when they returned from their day jobs that evening.

Now imagine, say, fifty thousand other homes in which working mothers are trying to raise fatherless children. After learning what had happened to Rosie Williams, how much less authority might they attempt to exercise over potential killers in their families?

HELLO AGAIN
MR. SKEPTIC:

Another white knight has launched a valiant campaign to checkmate a king-sized manifest of racism.

Please applaud New York State Assemblyman Edward C. Sullivan. He recently gave me a copy of the following protest that he had sent to Macy's department store:

Herbert Yalof, President   Sept. 2, 1987
Macy's
151 West 34th Street
New York, New York 10001

Dear Mr. Yalof:

In the August 30th issue of The Sunday Times there was a special section of Macy's called "Return to Class." In this section were ads for clothes, jewelry, etc. which can be purchased at Macy's.

I was shocked to discover that of 143 facial images of models demonstrating Macy's goods, only one was that of a black person—a seven- or eight-year-old boy.

It is astonishing that Macy's, of all places, would allow this kind of racial exclusion to creep into your advertising (I am assuming this was not done on purpose). Certainly more than one out of 143 customers in Macy's is black. I'm sure that more than one in 143 employees is black.

Unless all of us pay attention, and by "us" I certainly mean institutions that are as important and influential as Macy's advertising department, we New Yorkers are going to start slipping backward into the unintentional racism of neglect that characterized the early part of this century.

Black people have kids that go to school too!

Would you please inform me of the steps you are taking to make sure that future advertising bearing Macy's name reflects among its models a racial mix more in keeping with the mix we have here in our metropolitan New York community.

Thank you for your kind attention to this matter.

With best
regards,
Edward C. Sullivan

DEAR ADAM,

Having allowed you to peek into the blackest re-
cesses of my mind, as well as into the brightest, I
trust that you have seen what a mixed bag of
bones your old man has become. Sort of a hybrid
with some traits in common with Mr. Charlie. I admit it. Anything he can do, I can do as well if given
half a chance. In some cases, better. That is my little triumph. I have alternately played his games
and maneuvered him into playing some of mine.

My record shows a mix of wins, losses and draws.

Once you look closely, Mr. Charlie's overall performance is no better. He has taken his lumps from
the Russians, Arabs, Japanese, Chinese, Israelis,
French, gays and feminists. His impressive skein of
victories has been inflated by the tactical blunders
of his least-sophisticated adversaries. Yep. The misguided militants in the underclasses—those who
insist on fighting the wrong battles with feeble
weapons and, above all, a lack of imagination and
pizzazz.

Consider the inspiration Mr. Charlie gets from
his patron saint: the great P. T. Barnum. What a
clever impresario. His epitaph should have read,
"Are you sure this is the way to the egress?"

P. T. Barnum is in Mr. Charlie's blood. Which
provides him with the necessary chutzpah to main-

tain his position higher than the highest nonwhites. True, some wealthy, privileged individual blacks have been granted membership in the establishment. But we are talking junior memberships here.

Raw power. Control. Flimflam where possible. Violence when necessary. Those are his favorite weapons.

If we want to gain some of that power and control, we would be wise to learn from the white folks who have it. Take their Barnumesque approach, for example, to selling doughnuts, brownies, and other baked goodies in this classic TV commercial that aired last night. "For a limited time only," the avuncular announcer voiced over, "buy one, get one free." His correct assumption is that the muttonheads out there in TV land won't bother to extrapolate the relevant numbers. If they did, they would quickly deduce that the cost of one has been augmented to the power of three plus the advertising budget.

Deceitful, dishonest? Not by capitalist standards. As advertising guru Elmer Wheeler advised many years ago, they are simply selling the sizzle, not the steak. In fact, they have been getting away with scams like that for centuries.

How far wrong could we go by reproducing or inventing Yankee ingenuities of our own? Another definition of finesse.

Wouldn't you love to see fewer of our brothers trying to knock each other's brains out in the prize ring? Instead, wouldn't it be great to see more boxing promoters like Don King making millions by encouraging members of other races to damage one another's brains to entertain the masses?

In my fantasy, I see Black Barnum. An ex–pool shark, he has finally moved up to the heavyweight class of con artists. With the future of our people at stake, he cleverly takes advantage of Mr. Charlie's self-interest by offering him a gamble on a sure thing.

"Sir, the welfare state in our ghettos, which is costing you billions of dollars a year, has obviously failed. Your research for the 1988 fiscal year demonstrates that quite conclusively. Most of the taxes you paid cheerfully to help the underprivileged was spent instead to support the superbureaucracies that dole out the stipends. The figures show that roughly one fourth of the total is actually spent for rent, food, clothing, and other essentials. In other words, Mr. Charlie, you are being snookered in broad daylight."

Once Mr. Charlie buys that true bill of goods, Black Barnum slyly introduces a sweet solution. Yep, a sting. "There is a way to make those welfare billions do a heck of a lot more for the little people—for our country as a whole—if you let my nonprofit corporation help you invest those billions. Think of how much profit you could make by creating jobs and training the underprivileged to fill them. Once they are gainfully employed taxpayers, you can recover your seed money many times over by snookering and fleecing the suckers."

Trust me, son. Nine times out of ten, Mr. Charlie will take the bait. He also will take credit for the idea. No problem. Black Barnum will see to it that Mr. C. writes an overdue piece of legislation, casts a vote, and signs a check.

TO MY SON THE APPRENTICE CASANOVA:

So it's good-bye Sasha one day, hello Tammara the next. Personally, I like Sasha best; but your choice is all that matters of course.

Each year as you plunge deeper into the mysteries of love and sex, you confirm that your dad's secret wish on the day you were born has come true. The apple didn't fall very far from the tree. Invariably, you pretend to know it all when I offer to share my wisdom about the wonderful world of female critters. Herewith is a Baedeker, what you would have heard had you listened.

1. If you are curious about marriage, talk with a few of the boys who have had one too many.

2. Look for your second wife before you marry the first.

3. If you are a real man, women will go out of their way to please you; provided, that is, you not only serve a lot of home-cooked dinners with wine, but never let them clear the table or do the dishes.

4. If she offers to sing for her supper, you call the tune.

5. Guys who cook do not have to be great chefs. They are, in the eyes of real women, like dogs that walk upright on their hind legs: It is not that they do it well, but that they manage to do it at all.

6. Cooking is out of the question, however, until you have accumulated enough collateral to buy the best automatic dishwasher extant.

7. Don't bother making dessert; serve a feisty liqueur instead.

8. If you suspect that your libido is about to drive you into some stupid adventure, take a cold bath, then reconsider.

9. Never mind the size of her bra. Measure her C.Q.—crazy quotient—instead.

10. A one-fifth crazy lady is the best you can expect. She can be exciting and comfortable; a lot of laughs in and out of bed. Promise her anything except a written commitment.

11. A two-fifths crazy bimbo will start sanding your nerve endings within six weeks of the first tumble.

12. A three-fifths crazy sexpot will either forget to take the pill or otherwise set a trap for an untamed species known as prospectivus homosap.

13. A four-fifths crazy dame will eventually force you to drop her like a rotten tomato. She will then take off with a lot of your bread and self-esteem.

14. Don't take prisoners.

I am not making this up. Check my findings with any other old roué who has been there.

15. If you find yourself alone for the first time with any woman over fourteen, be sure to scout the nearest exits.

16. When a woman seems determined to change your personality or your life-style, you should make like a rustler with a posse on his trail: Ride on the far side of your saddle and sleep with one eye open. Otherwise, pardner, you're a goner.

DEAR ADAM,

I was boasting the other night, at a party for television newsmates, about my career move from *The New York Times* to Channel 4. "The Great Gray Lady" of West Forty-third Street has abandoned some of her scruples, but remains my favorite. Once in a while she comes up with a front-page story full of truth and quintessential ugliness.

> **DETROIT CRIME FEEDS**
> **ON ITSELF AND YOUTH**
>
> DETROIT—Shootings are so commonplace in Detroit that they are the subject of local songs and essay contests. On the average, one child was shot every day in 1986. . . . Detroit stands apart in the frequency of shootings involving . . . overwhelmingly, poor inner-city black youths. . . .

That article, by Isabel Wilkerson, also disclosed that many parents in the black community, being the most likely victims of black crime, were calling for hard-line defenses. "Like resurrecting old-fashioned reform schools, the death penalty and prayer in the classrooms."

I am not impressed by their tardy reaction. They

are partly responsible for the carnage. What disciplines had they been teaching their kids in the years before '86?

Nor am I enamored of the American Civil Liberties Union. Granted, they have done good stuff. They have come between a bunch of little people and a bunch of big putzes who were bent on attacking from the rear. What the ACLU miscalculates are the ultimate consequences of making everything softer for the bad guys, everything harder for the cops. Shouldn't it be vice versa?

In Detroit, one shortsighted solution was a landmark court decision. It knocked out the public-school policy of random searches for weapons without warning—a revolting development if I ever heard one. Today, the *Times* reported—after the murder of a seventeen-year-old Detroit football player by a fourteen-year-old macho idiot with a .357 magnum—the concerned parents are casting about for magic solutions. They are demanding that metal detectors be installed in public schools. They are gradually coming around to accepting a harsh reality: By curbing a couple of civil liberties that encourage disrespect and violence in some circumstances, they could prevent the murder of their children.

Go ahead. Blame Mr. Charlie for maintaining optimum conditions for breeding successive generations of black barbarians. Okay, feel better? Good. Now ask yourself, will any white person ever accept full responsibility for something that had been launched like a juggernaut long before his or her birth by Umpty-Great-Grandpappy Charlie?

Right you are. That being the case, shouldn't we reevaluate our conventional wishful thinking? Why not audition a couple of radical substitutes?

Let us consider what black parents could gain or lose by recanting just two flimsy notions:

(a) the fiction that even though their undisciplined nogoodniks were nabbed at the scene of the crime, they were framed and brutalized by racist cops;

(b) the mind-set of despair that can only regard black folks as victims who have many rights in this society but few if any responsibilities.

Do you remember my coverage of the Edmund Perry homicide in Harlem a couple of summers ago? He was seventeen; a rare black honors graduate of Phillips Exeter Academy in Waspville. Had he lived, Edmund would have gone to Stanford on a full scholarship in September. Afterward, he certainly would have been introduced as "the first black man to" breach whatever old barrier was being abandoned by Mr. Charlie that year.

"He was our shining star," said a mourning cousin. "Nobody in our family ever did what he did. He was going to change things for us."

Alas, Edmund Perry and his nineteen-year-old brother Jonah—a prep-school graduate facing his second year at Cornell—had thrown it all away. They made the dopey mistake of trying to mug a white undercover cop who could shoot straight.

Those boys were classic schizoids. Beneath the Ivy League veneer that they had acquired out of town lurked an angry alter ego: A slender black male approaching his twenties.

"They had me down on the ground," Officer Lee Van Houten had alibied.

Initially, I was as skeptical as a pregnant tomcat. Like the unsilent majority in the liberal New York media, I smelled a trigger-happy racist executioner.

Fortunately, my training under grizzled curmudgeons at *The Milwaukee Journal* and the *Times* had long ago shorted out my youthful inclination to put snap judgments on the record.

Following the N-B-C's of objective news reporting, I listened to counterarguments and weighed the facts. As the story expanded over several days, I was particularly moved during a candlelight procession one evening. Thousands marched to Officer Van Houten's station house in Harlem. Peaceful vigilantes demanding a legal hanging.

Outside the Twenty-sixth Precinct, everybody's stomach including mine rolled over a couple of times, reacting to familiar maledictions. The Perry family's black knight errant in error was C. Vernon Mason. He jousted once again with the invisible empire of the Klan. "Officers of the New York City Police Department, your arms and hands are dripping with blood!"

Right on, Brother Mason, the crowd roared.

As the homicide investigation progressed, however, twenty-three witnesses spoke up. Many were black and Latino. Facing a multiracial grand jury, they told it like it was. Yes, as the white cop had been saying all along, he was being choked, punched, and kicked when he fired. "Give it up, give it up," one of the husky young thugs kept growling, his arms firmly clamped about the victim's throat. Van Houten fumbled at his ankle holster . . . Pow! Pow! Pow!

The punk who had been choking Van Houten fled into the night. His brother Edmund lay crumpled on the pavement, his life oozing out through a .22-caliber bullethole in the stomach.

What a waste.

Edmund and Jonah Perry, while growing up on the streets of hell, had reached a diabolical conclusion that was shared by many playmates: The criminal justice system had deteriorated into nothing more serious than a *Gong Show*. Another racist institution that could safely be flouted and conned. Any halfway hip dude could take the fast lane into manhood by ripping off suckers.

What fun they were going to have after their first score, Eddie and Jonah had encouraged each other that night, when they could brag about it. The other tough dudes on their block would be impressed.

I can imagine those virgin muggers dreaming of going one-up on snotty pals who had ridiculed "the straight brothers." They probably regarded their attack on Van Houten as nothing more than an initiation ritual. A prank.

I have not told the worst nihilistic prank that so

many blacks are pulling on themselves these days. I am thinking of half a dozen punks I recently interviewed on-camera in the Bronx. Gleefully, they expressed admiration for a psychotic jailbird named Larry Davis. You may remember him from several headlines. He had been accused of exterminating at least four minority drug dealers as he robbed them, and later wounding six cops, who were trying to arrest him, in a shootout. Clearly, his young black and Hispanic fans had been taught by someone equally as loony to respect a macho robbing hood.

One of those punks came blustering on-camera uninvited. "Hey, man, talk to me. I once did time in the same cell with Larry Davis on Rikers Island. Me and him, we were like the two black musketeers . . ."

DEAR ADAM,

Since moviemaking is in your grab bag of ambitions, I have a favor to ask. Could you someday produce the ultimate video of my daydreams? I will lay out the screenplay free of charge.

In the opening scene, a handsome dude who could pass for my twin is doing something typically—what the hell, stereotypically—black and uncouth. The first image that comes to mind is flushing torn pages of McGuffey's Reader down the toilet while conjugating M.F. verbs in graffiti.

Presently, our antihero is airlifted to a TV game show. For one million clams he is required to find his own name in the phone book.

After flunking that racially biased test, he . . . ah, but why go on? I am confident that my son, who has learned a thing or two even without four years of college, can take it from there. In time, I hope, you will find the inspiration to get cracking on this movie.

When you are ready to start shooting, please call me. I could sign on as your technical adviser. Go for pizza once in a while, spring for drinks. Besides, you are going to love the Hitchcockian DeMillian tear-jerkian happy ending I have in mind.

DEAR MR. VIDEO PRODUCER:

Consider this review of my favorite old movie, *Sounder II,* as a personal challenge from me to you. My ulterior motive is altruistic: By the year 1990, you may be goaded into updating that quintessential black fable by producing *Sounder III.* I am convinced, you see, that the inspiring message in that heart-wrenching saga is the stuff that could guide our people from down here to way up there.

Never mind the fact that "Sounder" was the name of this poor black family's old hunting dog. The important fact is a classic illustration of what can be accomplished through sweat and black solidarity.

The story was set in the Deep South in the early 1930s. The Depression was a bleak reality. About twenty sharecropper families finally came to grips with their sorry plight. Impoverished and illiterate, they had been condemned to spend the rest of their lives doing backbreaking labor to help white folks get richer. Without "school learning," their kids—already toiling in Mr. Charlie's fields—would never know anything better.

Since, in that backward era, the ruling class in their rural county saw no need for a black school at any level, they were benignly counseled to forget about it.

Instead, however, those unschooled dirt farmers organized a task force; they agreed to finance and build a one-room schoolhouse with their own hands. Their strong commitment to helping themselves, despite overwhelming odds, earned respect and modest assistance from one member of the white establishment. Unfortunately, this was not enough to fulfill the impossible dream.

A series of setbacks threatened to block completion of the school. The task force ran out of cash and lumber. Credit from the white sawmill was out of the question. There was dour talk of giving up. Then Nathan, a stubborn black man with two young boys and a girl in need of that school, stepped forward. His one-line sermon ought to become our credo: "We ain't gonna get nothing done moaning about it."

Significantly, Nathan uttered those words as he was walking back to pick up his tools and get on with the job. "There is something inside me," he explained to his elder son in another scene, "that drives me to see this thing through. . . . Son, all I ever wanted was to find some kind of way out of working myself into weariness in the fields. I been dreaming about that since I was a little boy like you. A black man in this part of the country who ain't got that inside him, well . . . he's just walking around dead."

In the final scenes, eager black youngsters file into a rustic unfinished schoolhouse. Sections of the roof and one wall are missing. It is nonetheless certain that these kids are moving at last toward the mainstream. Their proud parents at the dedication ceremony solemnly promise the young black schoolteacher that some way, as soon as possible, they will finish the building in style.

Yes, I think *Sounder II*—released in 1976—ought to be compulsory viewing for all black folks twice a year. That is, unless my son the video producer gives them the option of watching *Sounder III* at the second screening.

DEAR ADAM,

Having been born into a generation that had no television as kids, I can sometimes see extra dimensions in the electronic images on the screen. The snob in me calls it learning through my eyes and years.

I invite your attention to the oral graffiti currently in vogue on every channel. Mostly, "Hi Mom." Occasionally, "Hi Dad." Athletes who clout grand slams, score touchdowns, or defeat Communists in any sport are the most active of these all-American vandals. I am ignoring the insincere show-offs in the stands.

Lady Jan agrees with my appraisal of public salutes to parents from otherwise well-trained children: Solid indications that appropriate bonds had been established between the youth and Mom and Dad.

When those kids had needed the modern equivalent of a trip to the woodshed, those parents were tripping, wooding, and shedding; they were there.

When those kids had come home from school with lousy report cards or accusing notes from teachers, those parents were schooling, noting, and accusing; they were there.

In other words, those "Hi Moms" and "Hi Dads" send a clear, important message to the rest of us: The most effective affirmative-action programs begin at home.

BRACE
YOURSELF LAD:

The renegade in me is loose again. Otherwise, I would not spout the following heresies:

1. In certain circumstances, racially restrictive housing policies—well short of exclusion—are desirable.

2. We should be careful about some of our demands because we might get them.

I was covering a federal court decision that outlawed racial balance quotas in Starrett City, a middle-class housing complex in Brooklyn. Judge Edward Neaher ruled that landlords may not fix percentages for tenants of any caste. That policy, he declared, discriminates against prospective minority tenants on the waiting list.

Many black families in Starrett City (22 percent) and Hispanic families (8.5 percent) joined their white (63 percent) and Asian (5 percent) neighbors in appealing the misguided judge's verdict. "Your Honor, the normal turnover in Starrett City brings in six hundred new tenants a year. The waiting list every year is roughly seventy-five percent black and Hispanic. It's not always the pleasant thing to recognize race, but this is the only practical way in America today to accomplish this goal of integration." The voices of sweet reason. It would be dumb to pretend that racial prejudice doesn't exist. Quotas could blunt the worst of it. Without quotas, Starrett City's rainbow coalition would soon be overcolorized. The annual turnover of white tenants would escalate. Mind you, more than a few whites told the court that they had moved into Starrett City to avoid bringing up their kids in a segregated neighborhood.

I see no reason to back away from the truth. From my first cheap room in the Milwaukee Kilbourn Hotel to my current pad on Central Park West, I have always shunned overcolorized neighborhoods. To live there, more often than not, would mean accepting neighbors who urinate in the corridors, karate-kick elevator doors until they fall off their hinges, toss garbage out of windows, and refuse to control their kids. Yes, there are some commendable exceptions. In fact, most residents would not be like that. The trouble is, it takes only a tiny minority to spoil the quality of life for everyone.

Ergo, I have decided to award the True Grit Medallion of Honor to Spencer Holden. He is president of the Starrett City Tenants Association. "Speaking as a black man," he told the judge, "Starrett City is the example to this country that integration can work."

Amen. Personally, I would vote for a Constitutional amendment, if necessary, to legalize quotas like that.

Once again I urge you to keep in mind what we have learned about Mr. Charlie's line of reasoning. The record shows that he is willing to negotiate almost anything. If quotas were sanctioned, he would probably say, "All right. Since the law says we gotta live with them, I say let's set a quota no higher than their percentage of the whole city's population. Like twenty-two percent." Believe me, Mr. C. is quite capable of espousing common sense like that while giving it the bite of an insult.

P.S. In discussing the above with David Diaz, my Latino running mate at Channel 4, I sold him on housing quotas. I did it with this analogy from my private theater of the absurd: "Sometimes to achieve a positive result, you have to start with a negative M.O.—like slashing the leg of a snake-bite victim before trying to suck out the poison.

DEAR ADAM,

Unless my sixth sense is totally out of synch with my funnybone, I have lately picked up fresh signals of intelligent life in two unexpected quadrants of the planet earth. One clan calls themselves "Four Black Clergyman." A larger task force is known as "the Association for a Better New York." The latter are a thousand predominantly white power brokers among politicos and tycoons.

Separately, at public events covered by this reporter yesterday and today, spokesmen for each bloc voiced a common belief: The time has come to try a self-interest approach to combatting racism.

The Reverend Herbert Daughtry, Lawrence Lucas, Calvin Butts, and Wendell Foster told a news conference that they had decided to personally round up young blacks to join the city's police force. No more picketing and chanting to dramatize demands for more blacks in blue. Their campaign, Daughtry promised, would uncover a pool of thirty-five thousand to fifty thousand applicants.

Aside from giving enlistment sermons from their pulpits, the four ministers have contracted to appear on twenty-two thousand recruiting posters; these are to be plastered in every ghetto. "I've been telling the police for years," said Daughtry, "that greater employment of blacks, Latinos, and Asians would sensitize the department to our community and help humanize it." Then, in a stunning about-face, he added: "I have to be consistent. If that's what I've been recommending throughout the years, I can't say no when they ask me to help find the minority recruits."

Don't get your hopes up, Tiger. I will give you ten-to-one odds on this bet: Rev. Herbert Daughtry et al. will have to eat a very large crow. They will hunt in vain for that legendary pool of minority youths who want to become cops. Instead, they will discover another crippling side effect of the shaky-black-family syndrome: Without the stable and disciplined family ties so typically enjoyed by the upper classes, there can be no such pool. It would be far easier, I think, to find thirty-five thousand disadvantaged blokes with felony charges still pending. Naturally, they would only be qualified to make police work, not do it.

In the other quadrant, I listened to the movers and shakers of A.B.N.Y. They were having a power breakfast in the grand ballroom of the Hilton. A lot of informal chatter at tables for ten about defusing time bombs in New York's ghettos. The main speaker was Governor Cuomo. Sounding more like Reverend Cuomo, he preached the worthy cause of extending helping hands in self-interest. "With racial tensions at an all-time high," he warned, "we should be thinking about root causes—such as poverty and economic inequities." It was tacitly understood that ignorance, incompetence, and nasty attitudes always came with that territory. "We should think in terms of providing more jobs, job-training programs, and day care to more people who work."

The optimist in me stood up and applauded. The white establishment seemed to be growing up. Less emphasis on putting more cops on the street. Hell, more cops had been put on the street. Yet the crime rate for blacks and Hispanics was un-diminished. Whites felt no less afraid.

"White flight" to suburban sanctuaries, the governor said, is no longer a viable solution. "You can't just keep moving from South Jamaica in Queens County to Hicksville in Nassau County to Riverhead in Suffolk County. 'Cause eventually there's Montauk Point ... the next stop is the water."

No more naïve appeals for ecumenical brotherhood either. Instead, Cuomo specified flatly, "You should improve conditions for these people out of self-interest. By the year 2000—that's only thirteen years from now—the majority of the work force in this country is going to be mi-norities. One out of two—half of them, at least—are being raised in poverty. Now, what kind of work force are you going to have in the years ahead? How are you going to make it without them?"

DEAR ADAM,

Forgetting for the nonce your current one and only Tammara, you undoubtedly have gazed across a crowded room, and lo! There she was. Miss Scrumptious. With your heart full of romance, you approached your dream. Then she spoke. "Can I ax if you be on TV?"

Professor Higgins himself would be wholly discouraged by that baggage.

I am talking about another offense that blacks ought to recognize as an unnecessary handicap: A flagrant disrespect for diction and grammar. Which strikes white ears as further evidence of missing necessities. An erroneous mind-set? Nolo contendere. I suggest, however, that, language standards being what they are, there never will come a time when the establishment will stop giving demerits to individuals who fail to meet them. Remember, the majority rules. We do not have the votes to legitimize black slanguage. If we did, the presidential brother could decree, "From now on, the word *ax* is in. Dat three-letter word which the majority can't quite get their tongues around is hereby degraded. Using it shall be deemed automatic proof of inferiority and bad taste."

In a lot of our households, sad to say, nobody ever urges a kid who has mispronounced or misused a word to look it up in the dictionary. There is no dictionary. There is no line in the family's budget for books of any kind. There are reasons for that, of course, but no acceptable excuses. If we wait for Mr. Charlie to provide the tools we need, our children's children will also be trapped in this awful status quo.

It is apparent from American history that previously despised minorities—Irish and Italian immigrants among others—began to improve their position much faster when they improved their speech. In other words, pal, if you sound as if you have the necessities, people are inclined to believe that you do.

In sensible households of any color, kids are taught the importance of making a good impression. Manners, speech, grooming, and body language are among the most heavily weighted criteria. As in, "Stop slouching and stand up straight." As a beneficiary of such harangues, I too have a thing about speech. I associate crude language with crude behavior. How about you?

Which brings up a couple of dudes I recently encountered in the subway. I was waiting to meet Lady Jan in the IND station three blocks from our apartment building one night. Except for a dozing black man in the bulletproof glass token booth, the station was empty. Enter two husky punks wearing loosely laced sneakers, apparently bent on jumping the turnstiles.

"Do you know if any cops be around," one of them asked, eyeing me suspiciously. My clothing and body language, I deduced, had caused them to size me up as an undercover cop. Pressing my advantage, I boldly strode to within three feet of their sullen faces. "Do you gentlemen have a problem?" I said flatly, projecting an image more dangerous than a middle-aged wimp. "What's your problem?"

Now I could see respect in their eyes. "We was just axing," the second punk said, "if any cops be staked out inside the gates."

I shrugged. "Could be." Yes, I had my six-shot automatic in my back pocket. I had no intention or desire to use it, however, unless attacked and given no room to retreat.

After wistful glances at the turnstiles nearby, these bozos began a slow retreat toward the exit. "Tonight, I guess," one said ruefully, "we don't be taking no train."

A good proud feeling came over me as they vanished in the night. For the first time in my life, I had not suffered such fools in cowardly silence. Then a worrisome question came to mind: Was this how Bernie Goetz got started?

DEAR ADAM
THE NEW
ADULT:

I have been meaning for some time to warn you about a subtle array of intellectual snares and pitfalls. Beyond childhood, you now are an unprotected species. Missteps can ruin your life. With all the printed maps and oral directions that you have been given up to now, you may feel quite prepared. I doubt that you are.

Lesson No. 1: Your maps include some miscalculations drawn by The Three Stooges. Almost every avenue, fast lane, and alley is either mislabeled or carries no label at all. You therefore must proceed at risk, my son. Don't trust any sign that says THIS IS THE ONLY WAY TO GO. Look for an alternate route that might serve you better.

Lesson No. 2: It is human to rely on one's own perceptions. Still, you would be wise to stop well short of ruling out every concept that challenges yours.

Lesson No. 3: Life and contradictions are synonymous. Sure, trying to live with contradictions can drive you bonkers. I can assure you, however, that you won't have any choice on that issue. In this higgledy-piggledy world of uncertainties, going bonkers to some degree is de rigueur. Besides, you will learn, to your advantage, that once your enemies are convinced you are crazy, they will be more inclined to leave you alone. Contradictions lend a certain yin-yang symmetry to all that we learn and experience.

Lesson No. 4: A crazy person with talent, money, or power is readily accepted as an eccentric.

Lesson No. 5: In addition to your maps, a whopping percentage of almost everything else that matters will also come packaged deceptively. Why? There is a long tradition among us foolish mortals to euphemize our errors, crimes, and fears. One shameful example was the advice of a White House aide, Patrick Moynihan, several years ago on the race problem. When the president asked what course his administration should take, the future New York senator coined a classic contradiction in two words: "Benign neglect." You probably were too young to notice when it happened, but Moynihan's euphemism became official policy.

Lesson No. 6: Before accepting or rejecting any label, consider who or what may be behind it. Punch up the suspect's rap sheet on your mental computer terminal. More often than not you will discover unsanitary self-saving motives. Reaganomics, for instance, has meant defining catsup as a vegetable when given to the poor. "Plea bargaining," as you know, means letting criminal parasites off with milder punishment than they deserve. In TV news, "live coverage" often means that the on-camera reporter is live, but the story is shown and told on videotape that had been shot and edited several hours earlier.

Lesson No. 7: Be especially wary of proposed quick fixes with mesmerizing labels like "open enrollment" or "community control." By lowering college admission standards to a militant black flag years ago, the liberal establishment created another mockery: A horde of illegitimate minority graduates, many of whom went on to become underachievers in various positions over their heads. They consistently "axed" the wrong questions and caused embarrassments to colleagues and employers, yet they were protected by civil rights directives. Lately, responsible educators have decided to go with a second opinion: What a stupid experiment that had been. Students who had failed to finish high school simply didn't belong in college.

The failure of community control over New York public schools is also being faced more honestly now. As you may have noticed in recent news stories, a move is quietly under way to transfer more and more authority from the thirty-two community school boards back to the central Board of Education, where it belongs. The good intentions of politically chosen community board members have proved to be poor substitutes for knowledge, experience, and expertise.

Lesson No. 8: Start compiling your own list of

euphemistic labels. The validity of your thinking and the quality of your life will improve immeasurably when you begin to make a conscious daily effort to call this, that, and whatever by its right name.

160

DEAR ADAM,

My faith in ungodly conjugations, in pursuit of black salvation, has been reinforced by a wily inner-city politician. Wait. Before you send for a butterfly net, please weigh the exculpatory details.

On a brief assignment in Chicago, I learned of Alderman William Henry's innovative response to the adage "It's very hard to be positive and poor." Twice a week, Henry turns his ward office into a "charm school." Thirty-three neighborhood kids receive free lessons in courtesy, etiquette, speech, and self-confidence. A hired consultant directs the curriculum, which includes field trips to restaurants to test their manners.

"If you know how to speak and how to handle yourself in a job interview," their teacher advised the kids, "you might improve your chances by impressing the person who can hire you.

"The words *please* and *thank you* can be passports to a better life."

I say it wouldn't hurt too if everybody learned to keep his/her mouth shut as often as prudence allows.

A dusky twelve-year-old girl in the etiquette class said with pride, "Miss Shelton taught me a new way to walk. Before, if you walked down the street, you walked all crazy, like trying to walk all cool. She told us how to walk like young women."

Alderman Henry, aware that image is very important in this society, wants tomorrow's image of our youth to evoke more respect, less repugnance.

Now I ask you, why did God fail to plant that little kernel in the empty heads of our delinquent parents?

Furthermore, why has God cut back reproduction of black role models like George Miles? A few years ago, at age forty, with a wife and four young Mileses to cover, he quit his job as a janitor and enrolled in a culinary school. Today, Miles is cooking on the front burner all over the place. "I work full-time at Altro Workshops in the Bronx teaching handicapped people to cook. I also work part-time for two branches of the International House of Pancakes chain—one in Hartsdale and another in Spring Valley, New York. On Saturdays and Sundays, I work for a convent in Yonkers. I cook for the nuns of the Sacred Heart Catholic school."

With all those kids, George Miles could wheedle handouts from the Feds, right?

He wouldn't think of it. "I want to make something of myself. You can't wait for somebody to come along and give you something."

I would add: Nor is it smart to expect an act of God to pay the rent.

DEAR ADAM,

Social engineers keep inventing substitutes for parental responsibility, but nothing works.

Their latest failed experiment was the Attendance Improvement/Dropout Prevention Program. Funded by the New York State Education Department a couple of seasons ago, it has just been dismantled after wasting thirty million dollars.

More than thirty thousand disadvantaged students had been chosen for this noble experiment—those judged most likely to drop out, cut classes, and disrupt the learning process for everybody else. They were scattered among a hundred medium-security public schools plus five halfway houses for girls soon to be grounded by motherhood. Special counselors were assigned to motivate that grungy lot. Their thirty-million-dollar pep talks produced no change of any significance, the engineers now concede. I could have predicted that. Official pep talks have to be backed up by authoritative voices in the home.

Half of the kids in the program, the final report said, failed to earn a single credit toward diplomas. They failed to show up every third day in 1985–86. The overall dropout rate remained at 30.7 percent. "The negative percentages were much higher for black and Hispanic students," said

163

a white voice freighted with apology. He euphemized their inferior performances by scrubbing the numbers from his text.

State Senator James Donovan spoke for me and the moral minority: "I've always been skeptical about projects of this nature in terms of their ability to encourage students to stay in school."

It comes down once again to the disarray of minority families, doesn't it? Is it entirely Mr. Charlie's fault that in 1987 more than half of black births were illegitimate, compared with only 20 percent twenty years ago? Who is responsible for the attitude of the welfare mom who said to her caseworker, "I've just had my sixth baby; what are you going to do about it?" Who should we blame for having two parents in only 50 percent of our households today, compared with 75 percent thirty years ago, before the welfare mind-set congealed?

I certainly cannot claim to have all the answers, my son. Common sense tells me, however, what ought to be the broad outlines of our game plan: We should concentrate most of our energy and resources on proposing and supporting only those projects that sensibly promise to help the black family to resuscitate itself. Clearly, it is the only social force that can lay down some hard rules for black youngsters and make them stick. Or would you rather experiment with more prison guards and electric chairs?

DEAR ADAM,

Regard this letter as a skittering chameleon of a footnote, belatedly attaching itself to all the others I have written.

Aside from our pantheon of black demigods in sports, there are less visible but more valuable role models out there, in politics, commerce, and hi-tech industry.

You probably could pass a quiz in which the answers would be Michael Jackson, Jesse Jackson, and Andrew Young. But what have you heard about the top one hundred black-owned business firms in 1987? I am not talking bootblack stands and gypsy cabs. I am talking banking, manufacturing, consulting, insuring, and distributing for profit.

Guess which of the following corporations that you have never heard of are in the elite one hundred: Mega-Data Inc., LCL Design Associates, Inc., United Chem-Con, Input Output Computer Services, M & M Products.

Right, all of them. Collectively, the top one hundred grossed more than three billion dollars last year.

Having read the success stories of half a dozen black chief executive officers, I think it is fair to conclude that none of those entrepreneurs had "axed" for lower college admission standards or easier qualifying tests. Instead, by studying hard and working hard, they made it big. When you read their words, you can tell right away that these dudes have assimilated the prime imperatives of the mainstream: Knowledge, skill, imagination, sweat, and commitment.

I am reminded of President Reagan's commencement address at Tuskegee Institute: "If black Americans are going to progress socially and economically, they must become part of the scientific and technological revolution. . . ."

One of my black alter egos in print, William Raspberry, summarized our predicament best in a recent column in the *New York Daily News:* "The problem is not money, but values. Values have to be taught and reinforced over and over again. The moral order we call civilization is a delicate thing that, left unattended, peels away to expose us as the amoral savages we really are. Is that what is happening in our inner cities?"

The black American who ranks today as my number-one candidate for cloning is Barry Rand. At forty-two, he is president of the Xerox Corporation's satellite conglomerate that handles marketing, direct sales, and services of Xerox hardware, software, and otherware from coast to coast. En route to that pinnacle, Rand had earned a bachelor's degree in marketing at American University, a master's degree in management, and an M.B.A. at Stanford.

Recently, after addressing more than two hundred Xerox senior managers at a conference in

Rochester, New York, President Rand said in effect that his path to success had begun in his home. "My parents always had very high expectations [for their only child]. Especially my father. I tease him because if you brought home six A's, one B-plus and a B, he's the type who would ask why you got the B."

With a dad like that, scarcely any kid could manage to muck up his life at the outset.

DEAR MR. FIRMLY INTENDED TO VOTE FOR JESSE, BUT . . .

After reviewing your excuse for not exercising that right—an excuse unrelated to preventing World War III—I have decided not to forgive you. So, "Take that, you busy young blade about town."

This is not to say your daddy doesn't love you anymore. Nor do I firmly intend to evoke the cliché of guilt: "Your vote could have made the difference." Forget about it.

If I know anything at all about the right stuff that my son is made of, you will certainly shape up in time to do the right thing for the next bold brother who puts himself at risk for the likes of you.

Have you paused to ponder what "The Great Missed Miracle of '88" is likely to mean to our cause? I see it as a classic episode among documented foreshadows of history. Verily I say unto you: What this country needs is a bumper crop of missed black miracles like the one Rev. Jesse Jackson pulled off in the New York primary. By winning the popular vote in the Big Apple, "He proved," in the prophecy of an NAACP oracle Laura Blackburn, "that this city is ready to be taken over."

Wow! That's heady stuff. Scarcely any mental charade gives me more pleasure these days than supposing the political fallout—before the end of this decade, I dare to hope—from the inaugural reign of "The First Dude" in City Hall. Not that I believe that Jesse's clone would solve all of our problems. As former Mayor Wagner once confided over drinks at the Waldorf, "Of course this city cannot be governed. What you do is try to keep the lid on."

Right. Ordinary problems defy solutions because of the overwhelming numbers involved.

Conflicting interest blocs, living among one another, can rarely be allowed to prevail outright in any controversy. Either way you go means stepping on an astronomical number of voting bunions. So of course I don't envision our Main Man leading us in a moonwalk to the Promised Land. Hey, I really don't care a hell of a lot if he turns out to be a somewhat tacky clown—ineffective, divisive, and abrasive. Like Mayor Koch.

However, I would expect "Number-One Brother" to keep certain campaign promises. Such as promoting "a fair and just color-blind environment" by abolishing all affirmative action programs. Preparation, Ability, and Character would be reinstated as Vice-Presidents In Charge of Personnel. All over New York.

Then, in keeping with a promise that never had

to be made during his campaign because all of us felt it in our souls, he would stiffen and enforce penalties—to the point of becoming Draconian— for every violation of anyone's rights.

Our "Prez to Be" would inspire a Baptist-flavored revival of family pride, honest work, and peer pressure. Black punks would be called by their right names—ostracized and punished as they ask for it.

Succeeding generations, spawned in that propitiously appointed incubator, would bear large roles in shaping and directing their city government—their city's economy too.

By the year 2000, St. Martin Luther King and St. Malcolm X, looking down from celestial seats in the first mezzanine, could finally sing in harmony: "At last, thank God and Allah! They got up off their knees. They have rolled up their sleeves. They're going to earn their way to the Promised Land. Hallelujah!"

DEAR ADAM,

While winding down from today's adventures in news biz, I sipped a dry martini on the rocks and watched a private-eye rerun on Channel 9. During the first commercial break, another simplistic cryptogram from Mr. Charlie came blaring into my living room.

"Give a kid a job this summer," said a friendly voice off-camera. The screen was filled by the head and shoulders of a slender black male approaching his twenties. He had no lines. With a grateful smile, he shook hands with a white *gantzeh macher* as the announcer concluded: "Remember your first break?" Before the youth faded from the screen and was replaced by a dog-food pitch, there had been time to read the subtle message in his body language. His hair was neatly trimmed. His eyes reflected intelligence—not a smidgen of sullen hostility for whom it may concern. His jacket, shirt, and tie were cheap but clean and neatly pressed. If he had been given the opportunity to say a few words, my impression was that young dude would not have butchered English with an "ax." If he owned a baseball cap, he would not wear it sideways. Never would he scorch his scalp with lye-based chemicals to tell a transparent lie about his hair.

It was equally clear that he, like you, my son, was not looking for a free ride; he was looking instead for a chance to prove his mettle. Yes, this young man had rejected the counterproductive values of the archetypal slender black male. None of his personal goals called for ostentatious threads and wheels beyond his modest budget. Never would he boast of being on a first-name basis with drug peddlers and jailbirds. Nor would he attempt to bully his way into a job by predicting "a long hot summer."

I am not saying that the rest of us should also pose no threat whatsoever to the white establishment. On the contrary. Malcolm X and H. Rap Brown proved quite conclusively that having a few hotheads on our side makes the rest of us blacks look positively beautiful to Mr. Charlie.

I do believe, however, that if more of us aimed as high as that clean-cut dude in the public-service ad, when we fall a little short, we won't have to hit rock-bottom.

DEAR ADAM,

You were right to chastise me for having failed to come down equally hard on the other side's crimes against diction. I certainly had intended to; other things kept getting in the way.

As far back as memory goes, Southern drawls have offended my ears. Like fingernails scraping a blackboard. Any nonwhite who has lived in magnolia country shares my negative reaction. Some bitter experiences as a child taught me to hear that sound as a threatening mix of arrogance, ignorance, and intolerance.

My prejudice has been reinforced over the years by movie and TV portrayals of good old boys. A villain, you may have noticed, sounds all the more uncivilized if speaking with a cotton mouth when he utters such lines as, "Ah got me a real strong piece of rope heah if you boys decide ya wanna string 'im up."

You never hear a chap with a firm grasp of and respect for the king's English saying ugly stuff like that.

Even when a bona fide Good Samaritan speaks in that Deep South drawl, my back arches instinctively; something primitive inside me starts pumping adrenaline, gearing up for a counterattack. Try as I might to be objective, I seldom succeed.

Yes, that is one of several elements in Mr. Charlie's act that could use a little help from Mr. Clean. Otherwise, honest dialogue and brotherhood will have to be put on hold—until traumatized ears of my vintage have been mummified.

Another aggravating flaw is his unpatriotic reverence for alleged heroes of the Confederate States of America. Which I rail against four or five times a month in my fantasies. I see blacks and whites in a promised land of détente. Guilt and power are among the many covenants they share. Responding to an almost unanimous plebiscite, they finally enact an amendment that had been missing from the Constitution since I first read American history in elementary school: "Effective this instant, General Robert E. Lee, Johnny Reb, and the rest of the defeated Confederacy are permanently demoted to the rank of traitor. Ergo, every painting and every statue of these bad guys in gray must be suitably altered, but not destroyed. A hangman's noose around each of their necks—under tension, of course—would be appropriate."

Unless you are a good old boy with a Southern drawl, I can't imagine that you would have any problem with that.

DEAR ADAM,

The scourge of progress was very much in evidence today. Covering a ghetto story across the Hudson River in New Jersey, I again encountered a task force of ubiquitous pests who call themselves "social engineers." For the most part, they engineer fiascos. In this instance, they blew up a delapidated complex of high-rise tenements in Newark with dynamite. Boom, crash! The Scudder Homes crumbled into rubble.

Like surgeons, they praised themselves, they had removed what they called "malignant tumors." As if to say that crowding poor people into the Scudder Homes had automatically triggered antisocial behavior, such as urinating and fornicating in the stairwells. Under the master plan, those minority families would later move into a new and "significantly different" project: A complex of cheap town houses in a neighborhood of superblocks for the poor. Scale drawings on display showed three-story town houses with real keep-off-the-grass front lawns and barbecue grills on the patios. Does that sound like the work of serious artists?

You could almost hear the drums roll and the trumpets blare at the noisy demolition ceremony. In new surroundings, said the social engineers, no problem. The relocated families would promptly cease behaving like the uneducated, disrespectful, and violent neighbors they had been on their old stomping grounds. That old black magic, right?

Naturally, I suffered an attack of satobia. It was as obvious as a naked jaybird that the master plan would fail. Architecture per se doesn't create slums. Nor does it foster teenage pregnancy, crack addiction, and other pathologies common to the underclass.

Wasn't it obvious that the new buildings would house the same or similar female-headed families on welfare? Inescapably, then, swarms of fatherless kids would be left without effective supervision for long periods every day. Drugs and crime, of course, would soon sneak in small, feed on the misery so abundant, and grow to monstrous proportions. Eventually, the surviving, demoralized families would organize vigilante patrols—as they had in the Scudder Homes—too late.

DEAR NEWS-
BIZ SNOB:

Your diminished appetite for TV newscasts is not something that your dad takes personally. Well, maybe a tad around the edges. Your primary interest, of course, is show biz. Okay. I just want to fill you in on a significant development. Four black journalists have won a landmark lawsuit against the largest tabloid in the nation. The New York *Daily News* is guilty, said a multiracial jury, of "giving fewer promotions, less desirable assignments, and lower salaries to blacks" than to whites with more or less equal qualifications.

What does that verdict mean beyond this case?

President Albert Fitzpatrick of the National Association of Black Journalists put it this way: "I think it's going to have a tremendous impact in the industry. . . . It will make newspapers and other entities in the media take a look at how they are treating minorities."

White-print *gantzeh machers*, Fitzpatrick expanded, should make commitments to hire and promote qualified minorities for positions way up there near and at the top.

Amen. The embarrassment and heavy financial penalties imposed on the *Daily News* may intimidate other sinners in the same state of disgrace to repent and embrace affirmative action.

I salute the triumphant Black Four. Being qualified professionals—not quota freaks—they certainly have advanced our crusade. Therefore I want to offer sort of a positive disclaimer. In arguing for more finesse in our dealings with Mr. Charlie, I am not ruling out civil rights suits and demonstrations altogether. To paraphrase Chairman Mao, "Let a hundred other angry voices boom." I continue to insist, nonetheless, that if we want to protect our gains and batten them, we also should harass our nemesis obliquely at times on a different front.

Let's face it, brother. Overexposure on television has debased picketing, sit-ins, and symbolic arrests; these are now boring clichés. You can see white folks, their eyes glazing over, struggling to keep from nodding off when such reruns appear on the tube. Individually they protest, "What the hell, I didn't invent white racism. So stop blaming me for what the Ku Klux Klan and Hollywood movies did to your image before my time."

In short, pal, they have stopped listening to us on that tired old frequency.

On the other hand, they don't find court orders boring. Instead, they consistently crawl out from under and slither into new loopholes in the law.

Which illustrates that we are not at war with the dumbest members of Mr. Charlie's family, but the brightest. Their hidden agendas are amply supported by wealth and power. Their apparent advantages are amply supported by wealth and power. Their apparent advantages remind me of Damon Runyon's classic tout: "The race is not always to the swiftest, nor the battle to the strong. But that's the way to bet."

To offset the odds against us, as my old man used to say, we must not be single-minded, but less and less predictable in our struggle. "Like a one-armed paperhanger, you have to swarm all over the job to get it done."

DEAR STAR OF
THE SHOW:

Lady Jan and I are still talking about your marvelous performance the other night. With so many other admirers fawning over you after the show, we held our enthusiasm at half-throttle to let you enjoy the accolades of strangers. You deserved it.

I was awed first of all by the cast: Six attractive young females, on the poster outside the nightclub, with one handsome Adam. "How the hell did he manage that?" I wondered aloud as we arrived. "Look at the credits on the poster," Jan advised. I slapped on my reading glasses. "Un-hunh. An original revue written mostly by Adam with a little help from his friends."

Later, of course, I recognized your personal touch in the songs and comedy routines. While I didn't get the impression that you were ready for Carnegie Hall, you certainly showed a good deal of promise on every front.

On a deeper level, however, your almost flawless performance—grammar and diction in particular—shook me up. Having made such a big deal, in earlier letters, about minority slanguage, I was reminded of the struggle that I had had in bringing my speech up to television standards. It took the better part of two years. I am talking about a ghetto accent with Southern overtones—described by my critics at Channel 4 as "a lazy tongue."

So they hired a miracle worker named Liz Dixon to work with me, Gabe Pressman, Edwin Newman, Dr. Frank Field, and other imperfect broadcasters on our news team in 1964. I spent two hours a week with Ms. Dixon in her studio. Over and over we articulated a zillion variations of "How now brown cow" without using those words.

Gradually I learned to harden my t's, buzz my s's, and articulate my g's. The timbre and authority in my voice were amplified. My fame and fortune became permanently linked to more than a dozen voice exercises that sounded rather absurd. My favorite was, "Oooo as in twooo. Waaay as in gaaay. Waaah as in baaah. Woooe as in grooow." Thus spake your dad at least fifteen minutes a day for the next two decades. If I became careless about practicing, Liz Dixon had warned repeatedly, my lazy tongue would quickly revive old habits. Early on, I ignored my mentor; skipped a day or two here and there. ¡Caramba! She was right. Some words would come oozing out of my mouth with the speed and consistency of mush.

So I stopped working against myself, started paying my dues on time. Until you get those two clichés right, I learned, you cannot call yourself a grown-up. Once you stop working against yourself and start paying your dues on time, other useful clichés become possible. Like getting ahead and staying at the top of your game. As I said, though, good speech didn't come easy for me.

I have admitted all of that, my son, to say this: When I talk of urging blacks and Hispanics to work on mainstreamlining their speech, I am not talking broadcasting quality. Pear-shaped tones are not required. I would be happy if they managed to eliminate a mere two dozen of the grossest misuses of nouns, verbs, prepositions, and expletives that ought to be deleted.

Now, I ask you, is that too much to ask?

DEAR ADAM,

Fortunately for all of us, common sense—that indispensable adjunct to civilization—is very resilient. No matter what rigmaroles the bad guys devise to put it down, common sense keeps bouncing up, like an indestructible nemesis of the status bogus.

I thought of all that against the background of two illuminating footnotes to black history that made small headlines today.

A senior air force personnel officer, Major General Robert Oaks, explained to the media why integrating blacks into the military is so much easier than it is in civilian establishments. "Because the military is a controlled society," said the general, "the chief of staff can say, 'We are going to do this,' and it will happen."

The fact that white chiefs of staff have been giving orders to that effect—and enforcing them with court-martials when necessary—should be counted as a couple of Brownie points for white folks. The fact that numerous white civilians have been known to put themselves at risk for our cause should be counted too.

Despite such evidence of good faith, however, some of our kinfolks have suffered so much from the other kind of whites that they don't notice. They see a white conspiracy in every black failure.

As in today's announcement that eighteen black lawyers had been fired from the staff of the Legal Aid Society in New York, as required by law, because they had flunked the state bar exam. Twice.

As you probably are aware, most of Legal Aid's 840-odd lawyers in our city are white. Most of the felons they defend, at public expense, are black or Latino.

Vociferous members of the Black Redneck Society—tossing common sense out the window—demanded the reinstatement of the unqualified eighteen. Since most of the white candidates had passed that bar exam, they argued, it must have been rigged to befuddle the brothers.

Upon hearing that old refrain, Mr. Charlie and I suppressed our common urge to giggle; the long-range consequences of that kind of black logic was too sad. So instead of laughing, we raised our martini glasses for a toast: "Here's to satobia."

DEAR ADAM,

As I have pointed out before in letters and conversation, television's impact on our times is as yet unquantified. It is forever expanding, evolving new complexities in side effects and cultural feedback.

On the positive side, there was a rerun of a classic episode of *M*A*S*H* tonight. Inexplicably, it aroused my animosity toward TV programming *gantzeh machers* for not putting more stuff like this on the air.

Hawkeye and Trapper, treating a wounded redneck from Alabama, inject him with a sedative after surgery. He is going to be okay. Next, they collaborate on a black paint job. When the guy wakes up and sees his colorized face in a mirror, he panics. "Holy molases. They done gone and give me a blood transfusion from one of them." Zounds. Irreversible havoc has been wreaked on the rest of his life.

Hawkeye and his sidekick, enjoying their prank, don't even think of letting the "ex-white man" off the hook. Instead, they rub it in by telling him about the ironic death of Dr. Charles Drew.

In case you missed him in high school social studies, the brilliant Dr. Drew was an acclaimed pioneer in blood plasma in the 1930s and '40s. He was the first director of the first American Red

Cross blood bank in '41. The end came nine years later. After a traffic accident in Burlington, North Carolina, he was rushed to the nearest hospital. As in, "Quick, Watson, the needle. This poor devil needs blood."

Dr. Drew died elsewhere. That nearest hospital had been operating on the theory that the Rockies would tumble and civilization would crumble if one of "them" were accepted as a patient. All of the right people understood that back then.

Today, of course, the right people are still haunted by the symbolic lynching of Dr. Drew. In struggling to atone, they often do silly things, like naming a mean street in a ghetto for the victim. If judiciously manipulated, however, their guilt can become the fulcrum we need to move another barrier aside.

The crux, my son, is this: What our people need is a whole bunch of barriers to be moved aside. The way to increase the total is to educate more blacks to higher levels of competence. Aside from their contributions to society, such superachievers make impeccable martyrs. When wasted by white folks, deliberately or by mistake, we invariably collect the kind of damages that money can't buy.

So the superfinesse that I am trying to promote calls for multiplying our no-fault blacks. As you damn well know, too many of our current martyrs come with embarrassing credentials. You've heard their grieving families on the tube:

"Willie Dee may have been tough and mean,

but he would never stab nobody who wasn't messing with him."

"Why couldn't all those white cops with all them guns and dogs they had just arrest the brother? He only had one shell left in his shotgun."

"Just before he die, Bubba said he sorry he had to kill the old lady. But shoot—she wouldn't give up her pocketbook. Now, you have to understand how Bubba was suffering, man. He was in terrible pain; just had to get some bread so he could get hisself a fix."

Which reminds me of the common sense voiced recently by Lt. Governor Douglas Wilder of Virginia. In the midst of a scandal, he urged blacks not to sink their own boat in a sea of paranoia. "Don't jump up and cry racism when blacks in government are indicted for their crimes. There are no black public officials or white public officials under criminal investigation. A public official is a public official. A guilty criminal is a guilty criminal."

Now, that took guts; that brother had to face dissident brothers out there, in the simplistic world of let's pretend.

In my simplistic fantasyland, we consistently give the Willie Dees and Bubbas among us the disrespect they deserve. Meanwhile, we send millions of walking boobytraps, like Dr. Drew, out to bait the enemy, primed to blow up in his face. Think of the mathematical probabilities in our favor. Perhaps a thousand times a day, white folks would have a chance to pick on a distinguished member of our new breed. Pow, wham, splat!

I can see a montage of banner headlines:

BLACK VICTIM OF WHITE TERRORISTS
NIXES NOBEL PRIZE "ON PRINCIPLE"

PROBERS FIND NO LAZINESS, DRUGS
OR CRIME IN BACKGROUND OF BLACK
POET DE-RHYMED BY WHITE CRITICS

BLACK INVENTOR OF "SAFE CIGARETTES"
SNUFFED BY WHITE SMOKER FOR A MATCH

188

DEAR ADAM,

This letter is either a false alarm or a five-star warning. If you dare to follow your dad down the road less traveled by blacks, you probably can expect a heavy load of scorn and ridicule.

Sadly, the human condition, at this stage of evolution, is sorely freighted with the wrong stuff. Though ostensibly committed to truth, many of us remain prone to turn our backs on it—even when it illuminates flaws in our enemies as well as in ourselves.

Just the other day, for instance, Police Commissioner Ben Ward became a target of black-on-black wrath. He dared to tell a gathering of one hundred fifty black journalists: "Our dirty little secret is out of the box. Most crime in this city is black-on-black. . . . Most crime in this city is committed by young blacks under thirty years of age. . . . We are the victims and the perpetrators. . . . We should not try to hide it. We have to speak out about it."

Guess who was more or less expelled from the meeting of the Black Journalists Association, being hissed, booed, and christened "Uncle Ben"?

As he departed, a banner was unfurled in the audience. It spelled out a popular oversimplification: "If you're not part of the solution, you're part of the problem." I can think of at least one hundred fifty exceptions to that rule. How about you?

Wisely, Commissioner Ward consulted city crime statistics before repeating his heresy later in the week. This time, in the badlands of Brooklyn, he faced about two hundred black Baptist ministers. In a city that is 52 percent white and 24 percent black, he informed the audience, the breakdown on violent crime during the first four months of 1987 would have embarrassed the Black Journalists Association.

Murder—173 blacks charged; 111 whites.

Rape—289 blacks charged; 149 whites.

Robbery—3,818 blacks charged; 1,754 whites.

Aggravated assault—4,011 blacks charged; 2,889 whites.

None of the Baptist ministers hissed the top cop. They listened attentively as he went on to say, with apparent regret: "If you find your home burglarized tonight, it will probably be done by one of your neighbors. If you stay here too late tonight and then go outside, it may be a young black man who will try to hurt you."

A chorus of amens reverberated through the church. Those Baptists had been reading the *Daily News* and watching TV news as well as studying the Bible. They had also seen the drugs, the guns, the ignorance, and the violence that systematically was destroying their flocks.

It broke his heart, Ben Ward went on, to see so many young blacks in city jails and state prisons. His leather-brown face was a frowning mask of anguish. "The fruit of our community is serving time behind those walls."

As the crime statistics proved beyond a shadow of a doubt, truth is nonetheless relevant when denied.

In that context, I was not surprised by the nasty black reaction to Senator Patrick Moynihan's recent welfare-reform initiative. His bill would revise the welfare boondoggle that now encourages blacks to procreate and vegetate. Having babies out of wedlock and staying home with them instead of going to work pays enough to live on, better than some menial jobs. A hopeless black mother of four once told me on-camera: "I don't know no other way to make it."

In covering that sad story, I learned that sheer necessity has created nurseries in 17 public schools—more than double the number of facilities just three years ago. These 17 are caring for 290 infants while their unwed teenage moms attend classes. I am positive that I don't have to tell you which two ethnic herds now fill more than 80 percent of the available spaces in that program.

Wisely, their counselors stress the efficacy of earning diplomas and degrees, and developing skills to compete for the better-paying jobs out there. Otherwise—¡caramba! Down, down, down they fall into the welfare pits.

I also have interviewed scores of black absentee fathers over the years. "Since I can't find no decent job, man, my old lady and the kids is better off if I stay long gone from our apartment. The welfare pays 'em more than I could make." Which is true of underclass men with little education and no job skills.

Enter the good white senator. "My bill would offer a series of alternative programs aimed at strengthening poor families." A former UN diplomat, Moynihan did not say, "poor black and Hispanic families." On television, his Irish eyes smiling, he championed a saner approach to welfare. "To emphasize parental responsibility rather than government handouts."

Amen, Brother Moynihan.

If his proposal became law, all of our ghettos eventually might emerge from the triblight zone of welfare, crime, and drugs. Didn't I say earlier that without parental responsibility our hopes are next to hopeless?

Under Moynihan's new deal:

Child-support payments would be withheld from an absent parent's paycheck—just like taxes—or from his winnings in a crap game.

Single moms and dads under nineteen would be required to live at home with their parents.

Nine-month extensions of Medicaid payments would be granted to parents who found jobs that paid enough—under current realities—to disqualify them as legal freeloaders.

Compulsory job-training programs would be set up in every state for longtime freeloaders and new young parents without high school diplomas.

The New York senator understands that something has to be done to facilitate a massive black exodus from the pernicious state of dependency; that the best thing the government could do for the underprivileged—for the welfare of white America as well—would be to abet grass-roots efforts to reassert the hegemony of proud, independent black families.

You can appreciate, then, how chagrined I am every time I learn that black folks are overloading the welfare rolls in yet another city as wave after wave of new immigrants surpass them where it counts: In education, cohesiveness, hard work, and financial success. Asian and Oriental newcomers in particular pursue American dreams that are well beyond the demeaning limitations of welfare checks.

I am thinking now about Miami. I covered a night of black rioting, burning, and looting there during the Republican (Nixon) nominating convention in '68. After that violence, a few crumbs were allowed to trickle down to the ghetto called Liberty City. The pattern was repeated in '80 and '84. More crumbs.

Meanwhile, Miami's Hispanic opportunists—bolstered by enterprising refugees from Cuba, Colombia, and other economic-disaster areas—began to take over that city. Lacking bootstraps with which to pull themselves up, the immigrants exploited the political possibilities. As in, "Hey, mon, thees ees America, sí?"

More than 70 percent of the Cuban refugees became registered Republican voters. Simultaneously, they rolled up their raggedy sleeves and went to work. Cheap. Hotels and restaurants found it profitable to replace black peons—at $2.10 an hour—with Cuban peons at $1 an hour. Basic capitalism, not racism. Democrats, Jews, and other white liberals took flight. The Cubans rejoiced. Assimilating mainstream values, they expanded their horizons. Which also meant educating their children with the proceeds from their lucrative drug-smuggling operations and legitimate enterprises.

Earlier immigrants from elsewhere had shown the way—mixing hard work, sacrifice, and crime to promote themselves from the underclass.

Miami's unemployed black peons didn't get it, however. What was happening to them, they swore, was somebody else's fault. So they organized picket lines and vigils. Ho hum.

Meanwhile, the calculating Latinos were snatching the reins of power. Swiftly, they became the business and political leaders in charge. Cuban dishwashers, bellhops, and maids gradually disappeared. Their replacements were largely illiterate black Haitian refugees.

Okay. You are right. History was repeating itself, evoking memories of illiterate Europeans who had spilled into America and made it big by dint of their sweat and gumption.

No, I am not dismissing the fact that Cubans—like all the other nonblack immigrants over the centuries—could count on better breaks from the white establishment. In fact, rather than try to gloss over that inequity, I want to stress it. Given the overwhelming odds against us, it clearly behooves us to depend more on one another, to work together to manufacture our own bootstraps.

Isn't it apparent by now that the triblight zone of welfare, crime and drugs, is the worst slum in this galaxy? Can any thoughtful black person deny that our traditional strategy—blaming Mr. Charlie for everything while demanding ever-larger reparations—is irrevocably stultifying? Is it not clear that we are suffering as much from our own misconceptions and disrespect for truth as we are from Mr. Charlie's imperfections?

Our future, I believe, is not up to him. It's up to us.

DEAR ADAM,

Herewith is a classic example of "departee"—belated repartee that finally came to mind long after you had left the scene of your temporary triumph. In response to your challenge the other night to come up with "workable specifics" to curb the expansion of the permanent underclass, I formally propose a "McBAC" attack. Try to imagine how much could be accomplished by a Middle-Class Black Advisory Corps with units stationed in every ghetto.

I am talking about recruiting thousands of upwardly mobile blacks who have escaped from ghettos and sending them back in on rescue missions. With less than minimum wage stipends from the government, they would live on the wrong side of town from one to six months at a time in federally funded McBAC residences; these would be physically connected to McBAC education and recreation wings, offering the kind of guidance and care that underclass youngsters rarely receive in their homes. Here they would be taught the minimum necessities for making one's way in a civilized society: Manners and morals, reading, writing, arithmetic, and speech.

The length of service in the corps would vary, depending on the personal obligations and financial situations of each volunteer. Some retired folks,

for example, may leap at the chance to get involved in a new career, especially one that promises to save a lot of children. As for younger
recruits still gainfully employed in the private sector, I think many of them would be willing to live
on a stipend for several months if guaranteed by
federal law that at the end of enlistment their employers would put them back on the payroll—as is
currently required when employees return from
jury duty.

Furthermore, to offset legitimate fears of the violence that is rampant in underclass neighborhoods, each McBAC complex—in renovated
buildings owned by the city—would be protected
by city cops around the clock. At least two officers
on every shift. Otherwise, only suicidal middleclass blacks would join the corps.

Yes, an all-out McBAC attack would cost big
bucks. Suppose, however, it was financed by diverting at least half of the current welfare budget? In
the long run, that investment would reap priceless
benefits for this country as a whole. Which makes
the kind of sense that probably would move many
wealthy corporations, labor unions, and other institutions to contribute money, matériel, and expertise to McBAC. Why? Because the alternatives
would cost a great deal more, in blood and tears
as well as money. You see, unless McBAC can demobilize most of the loose cannons in steerage,
the good ship America inevitably will be sunk.

Facing that frightening probability, first-class
passengers will soon feel sufficiently threatened to

adopt some barbaric strategies in self-defense—like curtailing the rights, space, and peregrinations of the underclass, while expanding the brigs and the legal rationales for shooting potential mutineers in advance.

So let's go to where the trouble is and take the "shoot" out of trouble. Let's try a rescue mission.

DEAR ADAM,

I was too choked up with pride to allow my heart to speak aloud at the dinner table last night. Not every father gets to witness his son's final passage into manhood.

As you filled me in on your video-making project, I was really impressed by your sensible game plan: A twenty-minute feature relying 30 percent on imagination, 30 percent on balls, and 40 percent on hard work. Your business sense also surprised me. The trades and finesses that you have devised to finance your venture—except for props and costumes—seem perfectly legal and ethical.

It was your quiet rejection of my offer to write you a check for the difference that got to me. "Thanks, Dad, but I think I can handle this myself."

Go get 'em, Tiger. Look out world.

I breathe easier. You seem quite capable of advancing your best ideas. It is clear that you know the parameters of the hostile and friendly quadrants of the universe. You will not be emasculated. Nor will you suffer more losses than wins in any competition that is anywhere close to being fair. Like your granddad, you think in terms of creating an edge for yourself and using it.

Thus relieved, I can double my attention elsewhere. Specifically to counseling minority kids who are getting off to a bad start on the wrong foot. Brings us right back to Square One, does it not? Their future hinges mainly on our collective efforts to stabilize the black family and galvanize it with old-fashioned middle-class moxie. If the devil himself would guarantee that kind of tomorrow, I would gladly emcee his annual testimonial dinner.

What the luckiest blacks among us have in common, aside from higher educations, includes a no-nonsense grasp of basic facts; meaning, what's really going on around us.

In my case, I have learned to trust a tested premise: We learn by examining bits and pieces of experience, comparing the old with the new, then gradually rearranging our concepts. Eventually we create a unique collage that makes better sense to us, and will someday, we hope, to the world.

Which compels me to keep striving to help create the promised land in my fantasy. It is a place where manhood has been redefined as a reasonable facsimile of gentlemanly conduct. Truth is an echo that resonates with one's dreams. No one feels the compulsion to advertise their rage by dreadlocking or cornbreading their hair. All of our children have one set of parents and three pairs of shoes. Correct posture means standing on one's hind legs—prepared to fight, negotiate, or compromise. Every family trains its young to follow footsteps that lead to the winner's circle. Rednecks—black and white—have been shamed into exile. Old enemies can laugh at themselves and one another. The battle of the sexes is deescalating, resembling an MGM musical of the fifties. The last place anyone wants to be is on the dole.

It is that vision, my son, that inspires me to risk the wrath of my orthodox God-fearing kinfolks. From here on out, I intend to lecture and lobby for antiwelfare and anticonfrontational black strategies. With luck, I might stimulate debates over dozens of new ideas that are clearly superior to my suggestions.

Imagine Black Barnum trying to sell my renegade a priori notion: "Hey, brothers and sisters, listen up. How would you like to run a little scam on Mr. Charlie? Well, there is a way. All you have to do is clean up your act, then put together a better act with more possibilities. He won't be expecting a blitz like that from his blind side, right? Hee, ho, haw. Mr. Charlie would never know what hit him."

Finesse, son, finesse.